SHADES OF *BROWN*
New Perspectives on
School Desegregation

Earlier versions of the essays in this book were read at a symposium, "Elusive Equality: Searching for Remedies in *Brown*," held at the Harvard Law School in the Fall of 1978.

The essays in this book were written with the support of funds provided by the Harvard Law School and the Harvard University Press. Publication was made possible by a grant from the Ford Foundation.

CONTRIBUTORS

Derrick Bell
Robert L. Carter
Ronald R. Edmonds
Alan David Freeman
Charles R. Lawrence
Sara Lawrence Lightfoot
Diane Ravitch

SHADES OF *BROWN*
New Perspectives on School Desegregation

Edited by

Derrick Bell

Dean
University of Oregon Law School

Teachers College
Columbia University
New York and London, 1980

Library of Congress Cataloging in Publication Data

Main entry under title:

Shades of Brown.

"Earlier versions of the essays . . . were read at a symposium . . . held at the Harvard Law School, in the Fall of 1978."
    Includes index.
    1. School integration—United States—Addresses, essays, lecture. 2. Discrimination in Education—Law and legislation—United States—Addresses, essays, lectures. I. Bell, Derrick A.
LC214.2.S5   370.19'342'0973   80-21877

ISBN 0-8077-2595-1

1 2 3 4 5 6 7 8 9   86 85 84 83 82 81 80

Manufactured in the United States of America

Contents

INTRODUCTION

For almost 50 years, or at least since NAACP lawyers in the 1930s began the long series of challenges to racial segregation that led in 1954 to the Supreme Court's decision in *Brown* v. *Board of Education,* the civil rights movement has been dominated by an integration ideology. The doctrine was born out of the fervor of those who espoused an end to discrimination based on race, and who believed this end could be obtained only when blacks were so thoroughly interspersed in the society, skin color would be as irrelevant as hair color.

The integration ideology served functions quite similar to a religion. It was addressed at an identified evil, was based on and upheld acknowledged moral values, and it sought a goal that seemed no less desirable because no one knew how it could be attained.

Over time, several different sectarian models could be discerned in the tactics adopted by those committed to the integration ideology. For some, the courts were the temples, and law the bible that would guide the way to the integration ideal. Others eschewed the courts, adhering instead to policies of peaceful protest; and still others valued the divine leverage of disruption, expecting to provoke violence by racists that would further integration goals. All but a few, though, envisioned realization of the integration goal within the existing economic and political structure of the society. America was to be transformed, not remade.

As with other religions, apostles of the integration ideology have had their faith tested by persecution. And they have responded with courage and commitment. In this process, many have suffered, and some have been martyred to the cause. A few of these have received de facto canonization. Because some have died and many have sacrificed, it is a critical item of faith for the integration ideology that the possibility of failure is not mentioned and the righteousness of the integration goal is not questioned.

Those who would perpetrate racial discrimination in either discrete or discreet forms have attacked the integration ideology so force-fully that the movement's priests have long viewed all criticism as hostility and all critics as enemies. Because the struggle to end racism has been so difficult, most who harbored reservations about integra-tion strategies remained silent. They feared that voicing their views would give aid and comfort to racists or appear an unintended re-pudiation of those who believed that integration was the only antidote to racism.

The absence of positive criticism has taken its toll in several areas of civil rights activity, but nowhere has the damage been more appa-rent than in school desegregation. If the integration ideology can be compared to a religion, school desegregation is the twentieth-century equivalent of the Christian Crusades. Issues that were once clear are now hopelessly confused, and goals that seemed reasonable have be-come unattainable. Neither group alliances that seemed permanent nor judicial support that was once so dependable have survived the clatter of conflicting interests. Worst of all, most black and other nonwhite children remain in schools that are mainly separate and predictably unequal.

The *Brown* decision has accomplished much that is worthwhile, but the twenty-fifth anniversary of that decision has come and gone, leaving in its wake more basis for commiseration than celebration. More than half of the nation's seven million black students reside in the 100 largest school districts. Over two million of these black children attend schools in the nation's twenty largest urban districts. Nine out of ten of them are attending predominantly black schools. The twenty largest districts average about 60 percent nonwhite, and many major districts, like Atlanta, Detroit, and Chicago, are more than 80 percent nonwhite. Many smaller districts are also becoming mainly black and Hispanic. Even where desegregation has occurred, there are serious problems of resegregation, and of continuing discrimination. Black students are stuck in dead-end courses and classes. Far larger numbers of black than white students are suspended or expelled. Harassment and physical attack remain serious problems. Worst of all, there is little hard evidence of overall educational improvement for blacks in de-segregated schools.

Integration, good or bad, is becoming harder and harder to obtain in those very districts where most minority kids live. The white middle class is disappearing from urban school systems. Whether or not its disappearance is "white flight" precipitated by school desegregation orders involves us unnecessarily in a long-standing debate that, to my knowledge, has not eased the rapidly declining white population by even a single percentage point.

The once supportive Supreme Court has lost its early enthusiasm for implementing what is likely its best-known decision. For a myriad of reasons skillfully assessed in the essays gathered in this book, remedies that once seemed quite capable of reaching even the most remote results of segregation are no longer available. Leaders of the traditional civil rights groups remain undaunted. They press on, convinced that without integration, there can be no truly effective education for minority children. But many black parents are disenchanted and have lost faith in the integration ideology. Equality, particularly educational equality, has proven elusive. But, if lost, it has not been abandoned by those who view education as the best hope for rescuing the masses of blacks now on the wrong side of that growing gap between those who have and those who have not. The long-term implications for blacks and this country if educational opportunity is not realized are painful to contemplate. It is for that reason that the essays published here seek to uncover remedies supported by *Brown* along heretofore uncharted routes.

I would expect, based on a decade of civil-rights litigation followed by another decade of civil rights writing, that the essays in this book will not be acclaimed by either opponents or proponents of racial balance-oriented school desegregation remedies. In most cases opponents are hostile to any policy that will alter the existing public school structure that provides the major share of resources to white children. Racial balance proponents, on the other hand, are convinced that unless black children attend school with whites, the essential benefit of *Brown* cannot be realized. For them, even the most effectively functioning black school is simply a segregated institution.

For those attuned to the either-or poles of the long-running busing debate, the positions urged in these essays may seem strange, unorthodox, even reckless. But it is out of just such unorthodoxy that effective review of existing policies can take place, and new means and more appropriate policies may be evolved. Given the current state of school desegregation efforts, even dissonant debate cannot further harm a process that is steadily losing hard-won ground. Moreover, the dearth of serious writing offering liberal criticism of school desegregation policy constitutes a form of academic abstention that speaks more for the personal discretion of potential critics than the public value of the silence that so many have used as balm for their growing concerns.

Each of the contributors to this book has expressed perspectives on the school desegregation campaign that depart from the unwritten civil rights Commandment: Thou shalt not publicly criticize. In doing so, they have offered new and unique insights on why progress has slowed to a halt, and how it might be reactivated. Some focus on the legal, and others on the educational, aspects of school desegregation. The authors differ from one another in matters of priority and emphasis but generally agree that equal educational opportunity is the aspect of *Brown* that deserves immediate attention.

Robert Carter and Charles Lawrence see the integration goal as worthy of continued pursuit, but they urge more attention to quality schooling for black children. Ron Edmonds and Sara Lightfoot are not hostile to the integration concept but see racial balance remedies as providing little of value and, when provided, posing more than insignificant obstacles to the effective schooling of poor, nonwhite children. Diane Ravitch, in tracing the variety of definitions school integration has held over the years, warns that the role of public education is limited and that to the extent integration is intended to assimilate blacks into American culture, it will prove, like segregation, simply another mechanism for subordinating blacks in the predominantly white society.

Using different approaches, Alan Freeman and I examine the jurisprudence of *Brown,* the economic and political factors that influenced both the decision and its spasmodic enforcement, and the very real possibility that lower-class blacks will never receive actual benefit from the decision that so many hoped would complete in 1954 what the Emancipation Proclamation began in 1863.

A final chapter provides details for a "Model Alternative Desegregation Plan" intended to achieve equal educational opportunity through effective schools rather than racial balance. Following a candid discussion of the barriers to, and potential in, the Model Plan, the suggested components of the Plan are reviewed as to educational merit and likely judicial support. The chapter closes with a survey of questions usually posed by critics of nonracial balance desegregation plans, together with appropriate responses to those questions.

I would predict that no one who reads these essays will come away unmoved. They are offered not as a total solution, but as a stimulant for debate and reconsideration. Many readers will remain convinced that the integration ideology is the one, real faith. To the extent that those true believers have answers to the criticism recorded here, their arguments should be more impressive than the "integration is right because it is right" responses they have relied on in recent years.

And for those for whom these writings open up new directions for thought or provide support for concerns long held but not previously expressed, it is hoped that the book will be a spark for further writing and advocacy. Even at this late hour, we may move school desegregation policies toward alternative visions of what *Brown* and its promise might still mean for those who need it most.

DERRICK BELL

CHAPTER ONE

It is significant that when we think of school desegregation, our thoughts turn first to lawyers and courts, and only secondarily to teachers and schools. Experience has shown that our priorities have proven as wrongly ordered in fact as they are in logic. Looking back, former NAACP General Counsel Robert L. Carter will suggest, in his essay following Professor Lightfoot's, that if he were now planning the litigation that led to the *Brown* decision, he would have sought out and relied more on educators. Professor Sara Lawrence Lightfoot, Harvard Graduate School of Education, shows how educational experts might have contributed to the case. She believes that the failure of civil rights lawyers and courts to consider how children learn, and the importance to learning of relationships between families and schools, virtually insured that the right to equal educational opportunity recognized by the courts would be lost in the schools. Desegregation plans, as a result, proved "simplistic and unrealistic arrangements designed for failure."

Lightfoot is also critical of the social science testimony that helped produce *Brown.* She admits it was dramatic and impressive, but since it was based on laboratory experiments rather than life motivations and responses, it oversimplified complex interactions that take place in schools and classrooms. Post-*Brown* social science research, Professor Lightfoot suggests, has contributed confused and contradictory findings by attempting to determine the effects of desegregated schooling while ignoring the processes of education and the interaction of variables that produce positive outcomes for minority and poor children. Little has been done to relate learning that takes place in the home with the teaching in the schools. But the efforts and influences of families, communities, and schools, Professor Lightfoot argues, must be harmonized so that the cultural and historical presence of black families is infused into the daily interactions and educational processes of children.

2

FAMILIES AS EDUCATORS
The Forgotten People of *Brown*

A MOMENT OF THEATER

When the *Brown* decision was handed down in 1954, I was ten years old. The memory of the moment the news reached our house is still vivid. The evening news reported the uncompromising, strong words of the Supreme Court justices that segregation in schools was illegal, unjust, and wrong. Jubilation, optimism, and hope filled my home. Through a child's eyes, I could see the veil of oppression lift from my parents' shoulders. It seemed they were standing taller. And for the first time in my life, I saw tears in my father's eyes. "This is a great and important day," he said reverently to his children. And although we had not lived the pain and struggle of his life, nor did we understand the meaning of his words, the emotion and the drama of that moment still survive in my soul today.

But even as a child of ten, I knew that I was experiencing theater. Pictures of the Supreme Court justices in their long, black robes seemed staged and dramatic. (I called them "the nine black men"—a habit I had as a child of labeling people according to the predominant colors they wore.) Their voices, coming from center stage, resounded with importance, and their words seemed articulate and clear. Somehow the clarity and decisiveness of their proclamation seemed to obscure the messiness, ambiguities, and complexities of the realities that they had had to confront in shaping their judicial decision. As players in the theater they rose above the muddled confusions of history, politics, and culture; they created an image and voiced a message that seemed pure to a child's eyes. I truly believed at that moment, that my black brothers and sisters in Southern schools would now have an equal chance, taste the sweetness of the American pie, and

3

learn to value their black skin, their history, and their children. I forgot momentarily the subtle exclusion and microaggressions that I experienced daily in my almost all-white Northern, middle-class school.

Why was there jubilation in my house because of a Supreme Court decision—rejoicing that was even experienced by my maternal grandparents who had been deeply affected by the vicious racism and oppression of their growing-up years in Richmond, Virginia? Part of the reason for their joy must have been their ability to suspend reality long enough to join in the theater: their own need to create a spirit of optimism in order to survive what they must have known would be generations of continued struggle. And part of their joy and resilience must have originated in the experience of unending oppression, a tactic of survival that seizes every glimmer of hope and endows it with exaggerated meaning.

The Supreme Court justices had spoken the word and the word seemed good. But how was the message going to be translated into the realities and lives of teachers and children in schools? Black and white bodies could be moved into the same schools. Children could experience greater physical proximity. Did any of this have anything to do with increasing reading scores, quality education, or greater self-esteem for young children? Whose agenda was being met, and for what social, political, and economic reasons? How was desegregation going to be accomplished against the massive resistance of threatened and insecure whites? Why did a large majority of blacks want desegregation? What were their motives, hopes, fears, and anticipated compromises? What would happen to the enduring relationships between communities, families, and schools as populations shifted and strangers invaded once homogeneous and protected enclaves?

Almost three decades have passed, and today there is no jubilation. The emotion faded many years ago; in its place, there is cynicism, withdrawal, and pessimism among whites and blacks. The drama, the clarity, the seeming consensus of that great day in 1954 has degenerated into hostility, confusion, and derisiveness among and between majority and minority groups. I will argue that it was inevitable, even predictable, that joy and optimism would dissolve and confusion prevail because the solutions proposed for the desegregation of schools were simplistic and unrealistic arrangements designed for failure. The solutions lacked an awareness of the complex, multifaceted processes of education and negated the strong, enduring, resistive qualities of institutional and cultural inertia. Most important, although the *Brown* decision focused on schooling, it disregarded the development of children and the perspectives of families and communities.

CHILDREN: THE INVISIBLE FACTOR

There was a bow in the direction of children and their needs in Drs. Kenneth and Mamie Clark's social science testimony. They spoke out honorably and forcefully for the vulnerabilities of young black children and argued that segregation was potentially destructive and distorting to the self-images of both black and white children. Black children, raised in ghetto areas, educated in segregated schools, and distanced from mainstream society, were likely to feel negatively about themselves, devalue their skills and competence, and denigrate their black skin. More significant, the authors claimed that these children when they reached adulthood would be less ready to face the "real world"—to move beyond the familiar ghetto style, idiom, and territory and walk gracefully and knowingly into the mainstream social, political, and economic institutions of society. On the other hand, the Clarks claimed that black children who had experienced more contact with their white counterparts at a young age and been less distant from pluralistic environments, seemed to feel better about themselves, adapted more successfully to the social and intellectual demands of school, and were less likely to misperceive their blackness (that is, wish so hard to be whiter and lighter).

Drs. Clark presented to the court evidence from a laboratory experiment—an ephemeral, unreal, and unfamiliar setting, very different from the contexts in which children live, cope, and survive.[1] And they extrapolated these findings to the more generalized, naturalistic settings of schools. Further research has offered convincing criticism of their methods, analysis, and findings. Despite the skepticism among other social scientists about the validity and replicability of their findings,[2] the Clarks' testimony was not only a critical piece of the *Brown* argument, but also a clear historical and political statement that galvanized the already-convinced forces and provided a comprehensive, intellectual rationale for desegregation. Once again, it reduced the great complexities to simple, understandable, dramatic data—all the more forcefully communicated by *black* scholarly voices.

One of the obvious interpretive difficulties with using the Clarks' findings as evidence of the value of desegregation for children is that their research did not describe the natural behaviors and perceptions of children but rather their responses to a contrived experimental task. Researchers questioned children about their choices of black, brown, and white dolls—a task that must have been perceived as relatively meaningless and disconnected to the real-life choices that children must make in their daily lives. Children were not questioned about *why* they made their choices, so the motivations, reasoning, and interpretations underlying their choices remained unknown. Adult perspectives and assumptions about children's expressed racial preferences may be crude distortions reflecting more about the prejudicial views of adults than the reasoning of children. Most critical, a laboratory experiment that reveals a child's racial identifications and preferences does not necessarily tell us anything about the child's interactions within the contexts of schools and classrooms. Are we to believe that a child who scored high on positive self-esteem in the Clarks' study would flourish in a desegregated classroom? Our analysis of the positive and negative effects of desegregation must not depend exclusively on laboratory data. Experimental findings may be useful indicators of children's responses to a particular set of controlled variables. But social context variables are strong forces that shape the roles children play, the relationships they develop, and the competencies they reveal, and these environmental variables must be considered powerful factors in the desegregation inquiry.

But even those sociological and social-psychological studies that have attended to social context dimensions and sought to document and analyze the effects of desegregation on the achievement and self-images of black and white children have not revealed convincing evidence, but rather confused and contradictory findings. Nancy St. John did a careful analysis of over one hundred social science studies conducted in the two decades following *Brown* that looked at the effects of desegregation on children (their achievement, self-image, and interracial attitudes). Dr. St. John scrupulously avoided issues pertaining to the constitutional or moral necessity for racial desegregation in public schools, and chose to focus on the more narrow, potentially more objective, question of the effects of racial mixing in schools on the children involved. Using a more circumscribed focus and dispassionate agenda, she chose her words judiciously and skillfully as she reported the unclear findings.

> On the basis of this evidence biracial schooling must be judged neither a demonstrated success nor a demonstrated failure. . . . As implemented to date, desegregation has not rapidly closed the black-white gap in academic achievement, though it has rarely lowered and sometimes raised the scores of black children. Improvement has been more often reported in the early grades, in arithmetic, and in schools over 50% white, but even here the gains have usually been mixed, intermittent, or nonsignificant. White achievement has been unaffected in schools that remained majority white but was significantly lower in majority black schools.[3]

Without getting stuck on the vast methodological and design in-consistencies that plague clear understanding and interpretation of the accumulated findings, there are a few persistent research barriers that have obscured our vision of children's experiences in desegregated schools. First, the great majority of studies that have been conducted to date have been shaped to correspond to variables that are testable, measurable, and quantifiable, and these might not be the most signifi-cant of meaningful variables to be looking at as we try to interpret the effects of desegregation on children in school. This is not to say that we should not be concerned with objective criteria that show losses and gains for children. We care if children score higher on achievement tests in classrooms where there are mixtures of blacks and whites, but because we have not observed the process of interaction and com-munication among children and between teachers and children, we are unable to make a judgment about what makes the difference, what produces the effects.[1]

Second, from the accumulated findings we do not have adequate longitudinal data showing patterns or changes in the responses of children as they grow older, have different developmental capacities, social preferences, and psychological vulnerabilities. In fact, in the researchers' search for *immediate* effects, we do not know whether the social rearrangements of desegregation were ever really given a chance to take hold on children. Are higher achievement scores in desegre-gated schools that are evidenced in the primary grades sustained throughout later elementary school and junior and senior high schools? At certain points in a person's developmental history might it be advantageous to be surrounded by people like oneself who might serve as sources of identification, mentors, and role models? In other words, perhaps there are a myriad of truths and solutions that reflect shifting developmental stages, individual styles and needs, as well as reveal changes in our responses to, and perspectives on, social and political movements.

Third, and most important for this discussion, research on the effects of desegregation has focused almost exclusively on what hap-pens *inside* school as reflective of the *educational* process experienced by children. The learning of children that occurs in a variety of other social and institutional settings is considered irrelevant and is largely ignored. It is important to distinguish between education and school-ing—a distinction that is often forgotten in a highly technological society where schooling is compulsory and taken for granted, where the family's educative function is often ignored or devalued, and where teachers and schools have assumed an increasingly dominant role in the lives of children. Education is a lifelong, cumulative, uneven process that occurs in a variety of settings with a variety of people.

In *Deschooling Society,* Ivan Illich tries to develop a language in which we will be able to speak about schools without constant recourse to education. He says, "I shall define 'school' as the age-specific, teacher-related process requiring full-time attendance at an obligatory curriculum."[5] And in harsher, more critical tones, Illich speaks of the damaging impact of the institutionalized indoctrination conveyed by schools.

> We have all learned most of what we know outside of school. . . . Half of the people in our world never set foot in school. They have no contact with teachers and they are deprived of the privilege of becoming dropouts. Yet they learn quite effectively the message which school teaches: that they should have school, and more of it. School instructs them in their own inferiority through the tax collector who makes them pay for it, or through the demagogue who raises their expectations of it, or through their children once the latter are hooked on it.[6]

Without condemning institutionalized schooling as nonproductive and antieducational, historian Christopher Lasch claims that families have a far more burdensome and complex task than schools. The study of families becomes critical to our understanding of the intellectual, cultural, and ideological socialization of children and central to our interpretation of social change.

> The union of love and discipline in the same persons, the mother and father, creates a highly charged environment in which the child learns lessons he will never get over. . . . He develops an unconscious predisposition to act in certain ways and to recreate in later life, in his relations with lovers and authorities, his earliest experiences. Parents first embody love and power, and each of their actions conveys to the child, quite independently of their overt intentions, the injunctions and constraints by means of which society attempts to organize experience. If reproducing culture were simply a matter of formal instruction and discipline, it would be left to the schools. But it also requires that culture be embedded in personality. Socialization makes the individual want to do what he has to do; and the family is the agency to which society entrusts this complex task.[7]

The family teaches what matters most, and the learnings are deeply ingrained in personal and cultural history.

FAMILIES AND SCHOOLS IN CONFLICT

For black children in this society, there is rarely a continuity between the profound and deeply etched learnings within their families and the social and intellectual lessons of school. Great disparities often exist between the style, values, and attitudes demanded by parents and caretakers, and those required by teachers. This dissonance is exaggerated and magnified by the conceptual frameworks, methodological strategies, and ideological inclinations of social science researchers. In fact, the disparities between the structures and values of black families and public schools have been a major preoccupation of social scientists who search for the reasons underlying the low achievement and depressed self-images of young black students in school. The scientific search, however, has not been dispassionate nor objective. More often, social science has justified pervasive inequalities, rarely challenged the asymmetric power between minority communities and schools, and obscured potential solutions by looking for sources of failure *within* families and *within* children.

Recent experimental work on the intellectual development of young black children, for example, stresses the inadequacies of their family life and the negative conflicts between black families and schools. In a study of language development and expressive styles of black children, psychologists Hess and Shipman reveal the classic modes of inquiry used by social science researchers. The authors claim that lower-class black children experience irreversible cultural deprivation because there is a lack of cognitive meaning in the mother-child communication system. They distinguish between the communication styles of lower-class and middle-class mothers, asserting that middle-class mothers offer a range of alternatives for thought and action (elaborated verbal cues) while lower-class mothers give predetermined solutions and few alternatives for consideration and thought (restricted verbal cues). Hess and Shipman use these two examples of a middle-class and lower-class mother preparing their children for the first day of school:

Middle-Class Mother:
First of all I would remind her that she was going to school to learn, that her teacher would take my place, and that she would be expected to follow instructions. Also that her time was to be spent mostly in the classroom with other children and that any questions or any problems that she might have she should consult with her teacher for assistance. To tell her anything else would probably be confusing for her at this age.

Lower-Class Mother:
Mind the teacher and do what she tells you to do. The first thing
you have to do is be on time. Be nice and do not fight. If you are
tardy or if you stay away from school your marks will go down. The
teacher needs your full cooperation. She will have so many children she won't be able to pamper any youngster.[8]

According to Hess and Shipman these excerpts reflect a disparity in
the quality and style of language and in the amount of instructional vs.
imperative information. More important, on the basis of this early
experience lower-class children are poorly prepared to approach the
task of learning in school while middle-class children develop into
assertive and reflective learners.

The Hess and Shipman data were gathered in a laboratory setting
where black mother-child pairs were directed to engage in preestab-
lished cognitive games, and their patterns of language interaction were
recorded and analyzed. Mothers and children were asked, therefore,
to enter an unfamiliar and alien setting, given an experimental task of
meaningless social significance, and observed and evaluated by strange
adults. No observations were taken in the naturalistic settings where
mothers and children usually interact with one another: there, the data
show correlations, not causality, between child-rearing practices and
achievement.[9] Even if we ignore the many ideological and methodological problems connected with this study, we must ask: To what realities are the mothers socializing their children? It would appear that
both mothers are equally oriented toward the constraints and demands
of school for their children. In schools, it is more likely that lower-class
children will be rewarded for passivity and compliance while middle-
class children will be rewarded for being creative, resourceful, and
assertive.[10]

The problem of language difference created by schools is intensified when one recognizes that language is not only a way of discerning
intellect and communicating information; it is a medium of culture, a
way of signifying one's membership in the community.[11] The language
of black children, therefore, is symbolic of social and cultural deviance
and becomes the basis of hostility on the part of teachers and rejection
of the whole educational process on the part of children.

Kenneth Clark's more recent work provides an important transition from focusing on the inadequacies of ghetto life to looking at the
structural and interactional patterns *within* schools that do not provide
supportive, nurturant, and receptive environments for poor black
children. In *Dark Ghetto,* Clark focuses on the rejection and hostility
that poor children suffer in schools oriented to white, middle-class
people and proposes changes in teacher behaviors, attitudes, and com-

petencies that would be supportive of the child's self-concept.[12] Most important, Clark rejects the class-bound, pejorative tradition of social scientists and recognizes the danger of thinking of lower-class life as a self-contained system, which would draw our attention away from the imposition of wider society. Despite his compassionate and insightful analysis, however, Clark still does not present the Harlem community in terms of its own social order, cultural idiom, or life-style. Harlem is described less in its own right than by comparison with everything that is nonblack and nonslum.

Although we recognize a shift of *blame* in Clark's analysis of family-school dissonance in black communities, he continues to be preoccupied with explaining the deviance and deficiencies of poor black children. The focus remains on the damaging impact of familial socialization and the resultant inadequacies of lower-class black children. The success and accommodation of middle-class black children is given minimal attention in the literature on race and schools. The range and variety of human values, attitudes, and behaviors within black culture is neglected by focusing on the poor and by defining their behavior in individualistic and motivational terms. Culture begins to take on a pejorative connotation as it becomes linked with poverty and race and the whole essence of inequality.[13] By attributing a distinctive cultural system to the poor, researchers have tended to isolate poverty cultures and focus on the alleged motivational peculiarities of the poor (self-indulgence, inability to delay gratification), rather than consider the various responses of people to the structural characteristics of the stratified social system as a whole.

EXPLORING DIFFERENT VIEWS AND NEW AGENDAS

Without exaggerating the power of social science and its impact on educational policy and practice, it is clear that research objectives and findings are intricately linked to prevailing social, political, and ideological agendas. Social scientists may reside within ivory towers distant from the stinging realities of urban schools, but the values, biases, and fears they project are part of this world. Even with the most objective and reliable instruments of analysis, they rarely escape their own histories, cultural preoccupations, and educational training. It is not surprising, therefore, that educational practitioners often find comfort in the wisdom of social science. Denying the critical role of families, emphasizing the irresolvable differences between black families and schools, placing the blame for the inadequate socialization of black children on the willful neglect or ignorance of their mothers, allows educators to assert the rightness and goodness of schools as the single, dominant learning environment. Teachers can rationalize their beliefs that lower-class, minority families are destructive settings that have an irreversible, negative influence on children, never to be undone by schools. After all, teachers in ghetto schools receive damaged materials to work with, and the best they can do is save a few exceptional students from the harsh realities of family and community life. Or a slightly more benign interpretation of the literature might permit teachers to assert that families are irrelevant and distracting to the educational process, and it does not matter what happens beyond the walls of the classroom. But rarely does the notion prevail that families are the first and primary educators whose effects should not be undone, but elaborated on, enriched, and expanded by schools. The sad irony of social science preoccupations with family-school conflict in black communities and the rationalized responses of educators is that education for the large majority of black children will only be successful when there is continuity, trust, accountability, and responsibility shared between families, communities, and schools.

This does not mean that there should be absolute consensus in values and agendas between home and school. As a matter of fact, conflicts between families and schools often reflect the cultural vitality and social dynamics of a changing society and can provide for the autonomous development and liberation of children. In his book, *The Temporary Society,* Philip Slater argues that in American society, people have endured a historical pattern of chronic change that has created an "experiential chasm"[14] between parents and children. This generational distance has, to some extent, invalidated parental authority and wisdom because parents have not experienced what is of central importance to the child, nor do they possess the knowledge, attitudes, and skills that are adaptive to the conditions of contemporary society. This child-adult discontinuity is viewed by Slater as a natural lever for social change in society. Schools (and any other nonfamily-based collectivity) have served the important function of regulating and modifying parent-child relationships.

> One segregates children from adult life because one wishes to do something special with them—to effect some kind of social change or to adapt to one. Such segregation insulates the child from social patterns of the present and makes him more receptive to some envisioned future.[15]

Dissonance between family and school, therefore, is not only inevitable in a changing society, it also helps to make children more malleable and responsive to a changing world. By the same token, one could say that absolute homogeneity between family and school would reflect a static, authoritarian society and discourage creative, adaptive development in children.

Discontinuities between families and schools become dysfunctional when they reflect differences in power and status in this society. When schooling serves to accentuate and reinforce these inequalities in society, then it is not providing a viable and productive alternative for children. The message of ethnocentrism is conveyed to parents and children when socialization, acculturation, and learning within schools are defined in the narrow, traditional terms of the dominant culture. The negative and paternalistic messages are also communicated when schools begin to take on the total range of familial functions—not just the responsibilities for intellectual and social learning adaptive to a changing society, but also the dimensions of primary socialization usually found within the family domain. Creative conflict can only exist when there is a balance of power and responsibility between family and school, not when the family's role is negated or diminished.

In an effort to initiate and sustain productive interactions with parents, educators must begin by searching for strength (not pathology) in children and their families. Teachers need to communicate praise and support for children so that criticism will not be viewed as a negative assault, and so that children and parents will not begin to adapt their behaviors to negative expectations. There must be a profound recognition that parents are the first teachers, and that education begins before formal schooling and is deeply rooted in the values, traditions, and norms of family and culture. Positive relationships with parents are not merely related to a deep appreciation of different cultures, traditions, and histories, but also are interwoven with the teacher's feeling of competence and self-esteem. If a person feels secure in his/her abilities, skills, and creativity as a teacher, then parents will not be perceived as threatening and intrusive. As teachers express the dimensions of personal authority rather than the constraints of positional authority, they will feel less need to hide behind the ritualistic barriers of institutionalism and professionalism.[16] There is need, therefore, to clarify and articulate areas of teacher competence, to make more explicit the spheres over which teachers have ultimate and uncompromising authority and responsibility and those areas where collaboration with parents could be an educational and creative venture.

What does this all mean for our understanding of today's joylessness and lack of optimism in relation to *Brown*? What does this mean in terms of designing alternative research, policies, and strategies for the future? It appears evident that the nature of social science research on desegregation and schooling must change. Researchers must begin to focus on the *processes* of education and begin to define the complex range and interaction of variables that produce positive outcomes for minority and poor children. These observations within schools must be longitudinal, allowing time for researchers to record the development of patterns of interaction between teachers and children and among children, and allowing time for the institutional rearrangements to take hold on children. The research inquiry should not be limited to measuring the positive and negative effects of desegregation, but rather to discovering what works educationally for children who have for generations been systematically excluded from the benefits of schooling.

The search for equality is elusive. But research on the effects of desegregation has also had a strangely elusive quality that makes one wonder whether we are asking the right questions or seeking realistic solutions. After reporting the value of desegregation in his famous study of 1966, *Equality of Educational Opportunity*,[17] sociologist James Coleman baffled and shocked the world less than ten years later when he claimed that court-ordered busing, designed to achieve racial balance in large cities, was causing a great deal of white flight from urban areas. Coleman, of course, was merely asking whether in the long run, "formal busing might not defeat the purpose of increasing overall contact among the races."[18] His seeming change of heart, however, was viewed by many as a moral retreat, an un-American gesture. A 1978 study by David Armor, using longitudinal data over a six-year period in twenty-three Northern and Southern cities, echoed, even magnified Coleman's trepidations of 1975.[19] There is increasing evidence of a significant linkage between white flight and forced busing.

Not only do these findings make desegregation of urban schools seem an increasingly unlikely and unrealistic solution, but they lead to a general disenchantment with the moral and intellectual nature of social science inquiry. We should not continue to get stuck in the quagmire of shifting findings, and the accompanying moralistic rage, about the pros and cons of desegregation and busing. In fact, both may be irrelevant and distracting to the effective education of children. Rather we must begin designing research and policy that ask what institutional structures and educational processes lead towards measurable, productive learning for minority and majority children. The *More Effective Schools Project,* directed by Ronald Edmonds,[20] is an important move in this direction. It is unusual in its optimistic search for examples of educational success, rather than its pursuit of pathology and disease in minority, city schools, and unusual in its recognition of the myriad variables that sustain educational effectiveness, rather than its claims for a single, magical cure.

Future strategies for designing more productive and effective schooling for poor and minority children must recognize the critical role of families as educators and the important relationships between families, communities, and schools. Being aware of the power and significance of families does not mean that schools should not be held accountable for teaching children. Rather the opposite—that once school personnel begin to value the significant place of families in the educational process, they will feel more responsible to the communities they serve and to the children they teach. Once teachers become more cognizant of the forms and styles of learning within families, education may be seen more holistically, and the medium and message of school can be designed to be adaptive to the values and idiom of community life.

I am certainly not arguing for the superficial interpretations of cultural inclusion represented in Negro History Week, now generously expanded and ritualistically renamed Black History Month. Pictures of Paul Robeson, Willie Mays, Martin Luther King, and Frederick Douglass are tacked on classroom bulletin boards. Their stories are bigger than life. They are distant unreachable heroes for whom children can feel deeply proud. But rarely are their lives honestly and meaningfully incorporated into the educational experience of children. Their pictures come down at the end of the month—only to appear next year, the same unchanging faces, a bit more tattered and worn.

Nor am I claiming that in recognizing families as educators, we should degrade or compromise educational excellence. This was one of the great mistakes of the sixties when large numbers of humanistic, liberated teachers, mouthing the rhetoric of nontraditional education, invaded black communities. They sought to establish loving, caring, familial relationships with their young black charges. Their goals were often laudable and worthy. Their hearts were more or less pure. But their hippy clothes, missionary zeal, progressive pedagogy, and playful style offended black parents who wanted a more rigorous traditional education that focused on the basic skills of reading and writing. In fact, if ghetto schools are going to begin to be responsive to parental values it may be that the authority structures, pedagogical modes, and educational goals of schools will need to become more traditionally defined with visible and explicit criteria established for child competencies. In the King School in New Haven, when parents became increasingly involved in the schooling process, they negotiated with teachers for more structured and orderly classrooms, and emphasized the rigors of academic work. As a matter of fact, some parents had become involved in the school specifically in response to what they perceived as a disorderly, chaotic environment that condoned deviant, disruptive behavior in their children and threatened the values that they taught at home.

But mere rearrangements in curriculum, teaching style, or staffing patterns will not produce significant changes in family-school relationships and community-school accountability. As long as power relationships between minority communities and white middle-class schools remain asymmetric, teachers and principles will not feel accountable to parents and children, and parents will feel helpless and threatened by the overwhelming dominance of the school. For a long time we have understood that the magic of suburban schools is not merely the relative affluence and abundant resources of the citizens (nor their whiteness), but also the balance of power between families and schools, the sense of responsibility and accountability teachers feel for the educational success of children, and the parents' sense of entitlement in demanding results from schools.

There is recent convincing evidence that redistribution of power and shared responsibility between families and schools in poor, minority communities have a powerfuleffect on teachers, parents, and children. Herbert Walberg found increases in the reading scores and intellectual skills of young black children in a large urban school where parents, teachers, and children drew up written contracts of participation and responsibility in the educational and schooling process.[21] *Time* and *Newsweek* magazines have reported stories of progress and transformation in all-black schools in Chicago's ghettos where principals and teachers began to demand the active and critical participation of parents in their child's learning and in school policy. With the support of parents, teachers were encouraged to adapt their styles of interaction and behaviors to the cultural idiom of the community.[22] And in the King School, in New Haven, the public, elementary school referred to previously, parents and teachers tell a long, tortuous, and inspiring story of getting to know one another, growing to trust one another, learning to fight productively, and finally building collaborative partnerships. Not only did the reading scores of children soar to new heights, but the essence of education was transformed by the presence of families within the schools.[23]

Schools will only become comfortable and productive environments for learning when the cultural and historical presence of black families and communities are infused into the daily interactions and educational processes of children. When children see a piece of themselves and their experience in the adults that teach them and feel a sense of constancy between home and school, then they are likely to make a much smoother and productive transition from one to the other. Black familial and cultural participation will require profound changes in the structural and organizational character of schools, in the dynamic relationships between school and community, in the daily, ritualistic interactions between teachers and children, in the consciousness and articulation of values, attitudes, and behaviors of the people involved in the educational process.

Finally, I would suggest that a critically important ingredient of educational success for black and white children lies in the power relationship between communities and schools, rather than in the nature of the student population. Mixing black and white bodies together in the same school and preserving the same relationships and perceptions between the schools and the families they serve is unlikely to substantially change the structures, roles, and relationships *within* schools that define the quality of the educatonal process. The nature and distribution of power among schools, families, and communities is a crucial piece of the complex puzzle leading toward educational success for all children.

NOTES

1. Kenneth and Mamie Clark, "The Development of Consciousness of Self and the Emergence of Racial Identity in Negro Preschool Children," *Journal of Social Psychology*, vol. 10 (1939), pp. 591–599; and K. M. Clark, "Skin Color As a Factor in Racial Identification of Negro Preschool Children," *Journal of Social Psychology*, vol. 11 (1970), pp. 159–169; and K. and M. Clark, "Racial Identification and Preferences in Negro Preschool Children," in *Readings in Social Psychology*, ed. T. Newcomb and E. Hartley (New York: Holt, Rinehart and Winston, 1947).

2. For examples of critical responses to Clark, see J. Porter, *Black Child, White Child* (Cambridge, Mass.: Harvard University Press, 1971); M. Goodman, *Race Awareness in Young Children* (Cambridge, Mass.: Addison-Wesley Press, 1952); and L. Sanders, "The Development of Racial Identification in Black Preschool-Age Children," unpublished dissertation, 1971.

3. Nancy St. John, *School Desegregation: Outcomes for Children* (New York: John Wiley, 1975), p. 119.

4. For examples of descriptive, ethnographic research that describe the *processes* of desegregation and its effects on children, see Thomas J. Cottle, *Busing* (Boston: Beacon Press, 1976); and Ray Rist, *The Invisible Children* (Cambridge, Mass.: Harvard University Press, 1977).

5. Ivan Illich, *Deschooling Society* (New York: Harper & Row, 1970), p. 38.

6. Ibid., pp. 42–43.

7. Christopher Lasch, "The Family and History," *New York Review of Books,* November 1975, pp. 32–33.

8. Robert Hess and Virginia Shipman, "Early Experience and the Socialization of Cognitive Modes in Children," in *Learning in Social Settings,* ed. Matthew Miles and W. W. Chartes (Boston: Allyn and Bacon, 1970), pp. 178–179.

9. For an excellent critique of the developmental literature on lower-class black children, see Stephen S. Baratz and Joan L. Baratz, "Early Childhood Intervention: The Social Science Base of Institutional Racism," *Harvard Educational Review,* vol. 40 (Feb. 1970), pp. 29–50.

10. See Ray C. Rist, "Student Social Class and Teacher Expectations: The Self-Fulfilling Prophecy in Ghetto Education," *Harvard Educational Review,* vol. 40 (August 1970), pp. 411–451; and Eleanor Burke Leacock, *Teaching and Learning in City Schools* (New York: Basic Books, 1969).

11. In "Illiteracy in the Ghetto," Jane Torrey distinguishes between the *structural* aspects of language (i.e., phonology, grammar, and semantics) and the *functional* aspects of language (i.e., the personal and cultural functions of language). Torrey asserts that the functional aspects of language have far more serious implications for children's accommodation to school than the structural ones.

12. Kenneth Clark, *Dark Ghetto: Dilemmas of Social Power* (New York: Harper & Row, 1965), pp. 133–148.

13. For an insightful discussion of the connections drawn by social scientists between cultural differences, poverty, and social deviance, see Charles A. Valentine, *Culture of Poverty: Critique and Counter Proposals* (Chicago: University of Chicago Press, 1968).

14. For a perceptive analysis of intergenerational distance and disassociation, see N. B. Ryder, "The Cohort As a Concept in the Study of Social Change," *American Sociological Review,* vol. 30 (December 1965).

15. Philip Slater, "Social Change and the Democratic Family," in *The Temporary Society,* ed. Warren Bennis and Philip Slater (New York: Harper & Row, 1968), p. 40.

16. Max Weber's classic distinction between *positional* and *personal* authority reveals the connection between feelings of individual incompetence and the need for institutional protection.

17. James Coleman, *Equality of Educational Opportunity,* U.S. Department of Health, Education and Welfare (Washington D.C.: U.S. Printing Office, 1966).

18. James Coleman, "School Desegregation and Loss of Whites from Large Central-City School Districts," Paper presented to the U.S. Commission on Civil Rights, Washington, D.C., December 8, 1975.

19. David J. Armor, "White Flight, Demographic Transition and the future of School Desegregation," Paper presented at the American Sociological Association meeting, San Francisco, September 1978.

20. *More Effective Schools Project,* principal investigator, Ronald Edmonds, Center for Urban Studies, Harvard Graduate School of Education, Cambridge, Mass.

21. Herbert Walberg et al., "School-Based Family Socialization and Reading Achievement in the Inner City," Unpublished Manuscript, University of Illinois at Chicago Circle, 1977.
22. "A New Kind of PTA," *Newsweek*, November 15, 1976, p. 105.
23. James Comer, "Improving the Quality and Continuity of Relationships in Two Inner-City Schools," *Journal of the American Academy of Child Psychiatry*, vol. 15, no. 3 (Summer 1973), pp. 535–545.

CHAPTER TWO

For many who participated in the long legal campaign that resulted in *Brown* v. *Board of Education,* it was the outstanding accomplishment of their lives. It is not easy to be objective about an event that has given meaning to your life. Understandably, most participants in the *Brown* victory are not tolerant of criticism. They are convinced that the case was properly handled and that the actual integration of students was its appropriate goal.

An exception is Robert L. Carter, now a federal district judge in the Southern District of New York, but for many years the NAACP General Counsel, and a leading attorney in the *Brown* litigation. Judge Carter, as readers of Richard Kluger's *Simple Justice* will recall, played a major role in organizing and presenting the social science testimony that, notwithstanding its deficiencies discussed by Sara Lawrence Lightfoot, served as important support for vital aspects of the *Brown* opinion.

In this essay, Judge Carter reaffirms his belief held at the time *Brown* was in litigation that until state-enforced racial segregation was outlawed, it simply was not possible to view segregation as only a by-product of the society's commitment to white supremacy. Now, he recognizes that the real evil, white racism, will not easily succumb to innovative legal arguments, and he urges greater emphasis on remedies designed to improve the calibre of education provided for black children.

A REASSESSMENT
OF *BROWN* v. *BOARD*

As I seek to assess the reasons black school children have benefited so little educationally from *Brown* v. *Board of Education,*[1] (Brown I) and (Brown II),[2] despite its being an almost total fulfillment of the strategy we had devised to reach that historic moment on May 17, 1954, it is clear that what we had won was only an engagement, albeit a critical one, in another phase of a long campaign. These negative comments are addressed to *Brown's* reach as a tool to upgrade the educational offerings accessible for black children. As I have pointed out in another connection—see Carter, *The Warren Court and Desegregation,* 67 MICH. L. REV. 237 (1968)—*Brown* did effect a radical social transformation in this country and whatever its limited impact on the educational community, its indirect consequences of altering the style, spirit, and stance of race relations will maintain its prominence in American jurisprudence for many years to come.

We are looking to *Brown,* however, to establish through constitutional doctrine equal educational opportunity for black children in real life. The problem, I now believe, was, at least in part, with our strategy. We were locked into a present that was already past, and the Supreme Court's announcement of May 17, 1954, was designed to restructure an era that was dead as soon as the *Brown* decision became law, although it was to linger on for at least two decades before finally giving up the ghost.

Come with me and turn the clock back 30 years, and perhaps I can help you understand how it looked to us then trying to look forward from the past. Although in its essence race relations were not fundamentally different from the present, in posture, style, and spirit there is a vast gulf between now and then. *Plessy* v. *Ferguson's,*[3] separate but equal doctrine was the national norm, and court indifference had

21

made separate but unequal the reality. Blatant, open, raw racism, churlish and uncivilized, was a fact of life in the South, and we were told that the South's outrageously demeaning race relations mores would never change. In the South black chi!dren were openly short-changed in per capita pupil allocations and in every other educational resource. We knew of no publicly financed segregated black school that could conceivably be considered the equivalent of its white counter-part. It seemed self-evident that segregation was the malfunction in the system that relegated blacks to inferior educational status and that integration was the only tool that could accomplish the necessary adjustment.

From our vantage point racial segregation—enforced separation, with its degrading humiliations—seemed to be the great evil that had to be destroyed. Segregation made it possible for majority whites to shortchange blacks, to deny them equal benefits from the public purse. Integrated education appeared to be an indispensable means to equal education. Indeed, to us equal education meant integrated education.

Of course, we were concerned with equal educational opportunity as a constitutional guarantee. We assumed, however, that educational equality in its strict educational connotations—with the emphasis on the quality of education—was the same as educational equality in its constitutional dimensions. Certainly that was the thesis presented to the courts in *Sipuel* v. *University of Oklahoma Law School*,[4] *Sweatt* v. *Painter*,[5] and *McLaurin* v. *Oklahoma State Regents*.[6] Beginning with *Sipuel*, we turned to expert testimony for the first time, and our experts' principal responsibility was to demonstrate that a segregated law school could not provide Ada Lois Sipuel or Heman Sweatt with educational opportunities equal to those available at the law schools of the University of Oklahoma or the University of Texas, respectively. We supported our thesis in those cases by measuring the physical facilities of the proposed black law schools against the existing universi-ty holdings and by taking into account the adverse psychological detri-ment that we contended segregation inflicted on blacks—all of which resulted in a denial of equal education. In *McLaurin*, we were required to argue that the unequal education there was per se the inevitable product of the racial restrictions imposed. You will recall that *McLaurin* had the same professors, books, and classroom instruction—he was given a separate seat set aside solely for his use in the classroom, library, and cafeteria. We could not argue that the inequality was the result of physical facilities. Thus this was the first case of pure segregation to be argued in the Supreme Court.

We adopted the same approach in the attack on the dual public school system in *Brown*. The testimony of our social scientists focused on the impossibility of providing equal educational opportunity in a system where racial separation was mandated by law. Accordingly, the basic postulate of our strategy and theory in *Brown* was that the elimination of enforced segregated education would necessarily result in equal education. And as I read *Brown I*, the United States Supreme Court was clearly of the same view.

Up to that point, we had neither sought nor received any guidance from professional educators as to what equal education might connote to them in terms of their educational responsibilities. We felt no need for such guidance because of our conviction that equal education meant integrated education, and those educators who supported us never challenged this view.

You might wonder, in the light even then of large-scale black and white school separation in the North accomplished by conforming neighborhood school districting to patterns of residential segregation, how we could have reasonably expected that in outlawing Southern-style school segregation, nationwide integrated schooling would result. The explanation is simple enough. Although separation existed as a fact in the North, the problem seemed to stem largely from housing discrimination. Moreover, there were no express laws requiring racial separation, nor was there the explicit shortchanging of blacks through per capita pupil allocations openly practiced in the South. Northern policies, therefore, seemed less pernicious, and in any event, we were certain that problems of school segregation would be cured as an aftermath of success in eliminating housing discrimination. In addition, the limited resources of the civil rights groups required giving concentrated focus to the legal impediments imposed by law in the South. Removal of the barrier *Plessy* imposed was our first priority. As long as *Plessy* remained the national norm, the North could perpetuate its own myth that it was more advanced and progressive than the South in dealing with the racial question.

In retrospect, it may have been a mistake to put all our efforts on Southern issues, but until we were able to dethrone *Plessy* as a national standard, it is difficult to see how progress could have been accomplished. At that time, moreover, we were not alone in the view that concentration on the racial practices of the South was the primary target. Both Northern and Southern white liberals and blacks looked upon racial segregation by law as *the primary* race relations evil in this country. It was not until *Brown I* was decided that blacks were able to understand that the fundamental vice was not legally enforced *racial segregation* itself; that this was a mere by-product, a symptom of the greater and more pernicious disease—white supremacy. Needless to say, white supremacy is no mere regional contamination. It infects us nationwide and remains in the basic virus that has debilitated blacks' efforts to secure equality in this country.

Even then, however, the present and future, which we sought to remedy with *Brown,* was past. While we were gaining in the United States Supreme Court some rather spectacular legal victories in eroding patterns of race discrimination in the South, these victories were being undermined by demographic conditions as a result of local school districting, neighborhood school policy and the rapid growth of the northern black ghetto, and the heavy concentration and containment of blacks in the public schools of the central city. While we were giving concentrated attention to securing a constitutional doctrine to bar Southern-style racial discrimination, the tide of black out-migration from the South was reaching flood proportions, with blacks settling in the large metropolitan centers of the North and West. At the same time, the introduction of labor displacing technology was rendering the unskilled talents blacks brought from the South of minimal labor value to industry in the North. Thus unemployment, underemployment, and unemployability were to become the lot of the new unskilled migrants that settled in our Northern urban communities, and quality education for their progeny became an indispensable need if the latter were to have any chance or hope of escaping the depressing fate of their forebears.

Moreover, our view about equal education and integration came under a more subtle attack when Judge Parker stated in *Briggs* v. *Elliott,*[7] (the South Carolina school segregation case on remand)—"the Constitution does not require integration. It merely forbids discrimination." This gloss was seized upon to support the notion that desegregation and integration are disparate concepts; that segregated systems need not be dismantled; that equal education need not be integrated education; and that school boards are under no constitutional obligation to take affirmative steps to comply with the constitutional mandate defined in *Brown.* Judge Parker's formulation, and similar tactics, delayed the desegregation process in the South but after more than ten years of waiting for *Brown II*'s objectives to be attained "with all deliberate speed," the United States Supreme Court lost patience and began to press for adherence to *Brown* by requiring that the dual system be dismantled in fact.

In the North, however, we had less success. The elimination of Northern style school separation requires a revolutionary approach to school organization that is fiercely resisted. And the neighborhood school policy, superimposed on wide-scale residential segregation, plus the concept of local control and districting rather than the statewide responsibility, and *Briggs* v. *Elliott* sophistry have all helped make resistance to Northern school integration respectable. First, the method used to secure integration in urban school districts is by busing, and resistance to busing has become a popular national pastime. Busing, of course, is inconvenient—at least when white children must board the bus in the morning. Initially only black children were called upon to be bused out of their neighborhoods. As the central city became more heavily nonwhite minority and poor, the busing of white children to formerly all black schools had to be undertaken to accomplish desegregation. Secondly, much publicity has been given to studies or views purporting to show that integrated education does not automatically result in an equal education in terms of results for black children. Finally, the nationwide decline in SAT scores has encouraged misplaced fears that integration of the schools will lower standards and accelerate that process. All of these factors have stiffened resistance to integration. Indeed resistance has been so fierce that today there are more blacks attending all or predominantly black schools than was true in 1954 when *Brown I* was handed down.

Raw racism, however, is no longer acceptable. Indeed, racism itself is no longer fashionable. Therefore, in a desperate search to find a basis for resisting integration, a basis untainted by racism, that resistance is articulated in terms of class differences. The argument is—and you will pardon the sarcasm—that since whites are so accepting of blacks who have propelled themselves upward into the middle class, the very noticeable majority antipathy to the rest of the black population must be because of their income and life-style rather than their color. There is, of course, some truth in the suggestion of class bias. Since the Kennedy administration, there seems to have been a national consensus that the country must take on the appearance of a multiracial society. Our institutions are no longer lily-white, and the process seems to be gaining momentum and increased acceptance. But this does not preclude an even more insidious bias. Blacks who become executives, legislators, judges, corporate directors, managers, university professors are those who have the background and outlook similar to their white colleagues. Yet, even these establishment blacks are deeply affected by discrimination. Only future generations of social scientists and historians will be able to tell us whether the frustrations blacks encounter within the institutions of power they now serve will produce a more embittered social pathology than the one resulting from the policy of exclusion that was the norm in 1954. In short, class issues do have a negative impact on black and white relationships, but the race issue—the color question—remains basic.

At any rate, while the pre-*Brown* thesis that equal education and integrated education are synonymous has never had a fair test, its chances of being afforded a just demonstration in the foreseeable future seem quite unlikely. Whether our views about the indispensable necessity of school integration were correct is really beside the point. Current public intransigence makes clear that we cannot allow ourselves to become the prisoners of dogma. While integration must remain the long-range goal, we must search for alternatives because the reality is that hundreds of thousands of black children are attending all black or predominantly black schools in the urban North and South. These schools are woefully inadequate and provide no tools that will enable poor blacks to become a part of the mainstream of the social, economic, and political life of the country. In the short run, we have to concentrate on finding ways of improving the quality of education in these schools, even if it means or results in less effort being expended on school integration.

The ineffectiveness of professional educators in specifying the educational package necessary for the black urban underclass to achieve equal educational opportunity has helped cause much of the present confusion and controversy. *Brown* surely must require the abandonment of all state educational policies and practices that result in a disparate allocation of public educational resources between blacks and whites. That would apply obviously to per capita expenditures, curriculum, remediation, quality of instruction, and intensity of academic pressures. It was in these areas that segregation had its most devastating impact in shortchanging black children. Equal education as education must mean at least this. Yet we now are reasonably certain that parity in these areas will not necessarily produce equal education for blacks. Therefore, it is now critical that educators articulate the indispensable ingredients of educational equality to enable judges and lawyers to develop an accommodating constitutional doctrine.

It is on the black poor and their education plight that we must focus our concerns. Without some concrete sense of what equal education must mean in educational terms, there is insufficient public pressure to upgrade the black urban schools. A definitive standard as to what equal education requires in terms of minimum educational resources that must be available in each school would prove a spur to upgrading educational offerings for blacks. In devising *Brown* strategy and pre-*Brown* strategy, in *Sipuel, McLaurin, Sweatt,* and *Brown,* we sought to measure input. If classrooms and schools free of racial barriers are provided, equal education follows. More recently it has been recognized that equl education advocates must be concerned with educational output—what is the result in terms of educational achievement of 3, 8, 12 years in the public schools. The emphasis now is turning to school accountability in requiring that X schooling should result in X achievement.

Public school administrators have been in the habit of excusing the system for educational deficiencies in the school servicing large concentrations of blacks. They blame the system's massive failure to achieve educational excellence in these schools on what is referred to as a "cultural lag" or "gap" among blacks; to the fact that the children come from nonverbal homes and, obviously, schools should not be expected to be successful in teaching these children the basic rudiments of the three R's. Judge Skelly Wright's portrait of the Washington, D.C., public school system in *Hobson* v. *Hansen*,[8] was a devastating exposure of the callous indifference of public school administrators to the educational needs of the black poor. In the belief that Negroes, particularly poor Negroes, were destined for the most menial occupations in the society, they were given limited and restricted educational opportunities and were not exposed to the more rigorous academic training available to the white middle class. The black urban poor is permanently trapped on the bottom rung of our society, with no hope of upward mobility unless the means can be found to raise the educational standards in the schools of black concentration.

While we fashioned *Brown* on the theory that equal education and integrated education were one and the same, the goal was not integration but equal educational opportunity. Similarly, although the Supreme Court in 1954 believed that educational equality mandated integration, *Brown* requires equal educational opportunity. If that can be achieved without integration, *Brown* has been satisfied. A number of blacks and whites contend that equal educational opportunity does not require integration. While I have serious doubts about that thesis, for the reasons indicated, their views must be given serious consideration, and to hold such views should not be regarded as treason in civil rights circles.

If I had to prepare for *Brown* today, instead of looking principally to the social scientists to demonstrate the adverse consequences of segregation, I would seek to recruit educators to formulate a concrete definition of the meaning of equality in education, and I would base my argument on that definition and seek to persuade the Court that equal education in its constitutional dimensions must, at the very least, conform to the contours of equal education as defined by the educators.

I am certain that a racially integrated America is best for all of us; but I also know that quality education is essential to the survival of hundreds of thousands of black children who now seem destined for the dunghill in our society. There are solutions, I believe, that can readily achieve integration and deliver equal education at the same time—state systems, metropolitan school districts combining the central city and suburbs, or placing clusters of schools outside districts on large campuses (much like colleges). The hope of getting approval of such remedies today through litigation or legislation is, I think you will agree, minimal.

Therefore, current civil rights strategy in education, it seems to me, ought to concern itself with many facets of educational policy— school financing, school districting, educational offerings, teaching methodology, and the delivery of services, among others. Although I remain convinced that racial separation facilitates discrimination, familiarity with the range of factors governing educational policy in the particular state or school organization should help prevent any basic differentiation in the delivery of services. Integrated education must not be lost as the ultimate solution. That would be a disaster in my judgment. For the present, however, to focus on integration alone is a luxury only the black middle class can afford. They have the means to desert the public schools if dissatisfied, can obtain remediation if necessary, and can get their children into colleges or some income producing enterprise. The immediate and urgent need of the black urban poor is the attainment, in real life terms and in settings of virtually total black-white school separation, at least of some of the benefits and protection of the constitutional guarantee of equal educational opportunity that *Brown* requires. The only way to insure that thousands of the black urban poor will have even a remote chance of obtaining the tools needed for them to compete in the marketplace for a decent job and its accompanying benefits is to concentrate on having quality education delivered to the schools these blacks are attending, and in all likelihood will be attending for at least another generation.

NOTES

1. 347 U.S. 483 (1954).
2. 349 U.S. 294 (1955).
3. 163 U.S. 537 (1896).
4. 332 U.S. 631 (1948), leave to file petition for writ of mandamus denied, *sub nom.* Fischer v. Hurst, 333 U.S. 147 (1948).
5. 339 U.S. 629 (1950).
6. 339 U.S. 637 (1950).
7. 132 F. Supp. 776, 777 (E.D.S.C. 1955).
8. 269 F. Supp. 401 (D. D.C. 1967), *aff'd en banc sub nom.* Smuck v. Hobson, 408 F.2d 175 (D.C. Civ. 1969).

Part II

SEGREGATION IN PERSPECTIVE

Diane Ravitch
The Viewpoint of History

Charles R. Lawrence
The True Nature of Segregation

CHAPTER THREE

The *Brown* decision and its aftermath, Judge Robert Carter
has told us, made clear that enforced racial separation was
merely a manifestation of the larger problem, white supremacy.
Diane Ravitch, a professor at Teachers College, Columbia University, traces the strands of white racism through American
history. She notes that Judge Carter and his NAACP colleagues
sought in *Brown* Supreme Court recognition that the Constitution is color-blind. Later, in response to racially neutral barriers
erected to retain segregation, lawyers sought color-conscious
remedies, such as racially balanced schools to provide black
children contact with the majority group. In a reversal of roles,
those who continue to resist school desegregation have made
the color-blind concept a chief argument. This resistance,
together with uncertainty as to both the proper role of the public school and the real educational needs of black children, has
slowed and now endangers implementation of *Brown*. Ravitch
joins Lightfoot in attacking social science findings that under-
value the role of black culture in effective education of black
children. She urges a definition and strategy of desegregation
that distinguishes and opposes all barriers based on race, while
recognizing and encouraging autonomous black institutions and
activities. The latter, she suggests, as well as policies designed
to insure black participation at every level of political and economic activity, are essential prerequisites to facing the more
basic challenges in building a stable, multiracial society in
which black culture is prized as a source of diversity rather
than viewed as a stigma by whites and a handicap to blacks.

DESEGREGATION
Varieties of Meaning

What's in a name? In social policy, the way a word is defined is far more than a semantic exercise. The definition of a strategic term such as desegregation is itself a statement of policy. Furthermore, embedded within a particular definition are assumptions, values, and policy goals. Thus, it becomes a matter of importance to make explicit, wherever possible, precisely which policies and goals are being advocated behind the neutral appearance of a definition.

Over the past 25 years, the words "segregation" and "desegregation" have shifted significantly in their meaning, and by examining these changes it may be possible to detect concurrent shifts in the direction of social policy. At certain times, these terms have had a meaning that then seemed clear. In the early 1950s, there was a general understanding of the meaning of these two words: "segregation" in school was a state-imposed policy of separating children solely on the basis of race; "desegregation," conversely, meant the elimination of state-imposed racial distinctions. These conventional definitions were repeated time and again in the record of the *Brown* v. *Board of Education* case. The way to end "segregation," as it was then defined, was to strike down all racial distinctions in the law as invidious and unconstitutional; a society freed of racial distinctions, it was then assumed, would be a desegregated society. These are no longer the definitions and the policies and the goals that are in common usage. "Segregation" today is a term that applies interchangeably both to discrimination against minorities and to racial concentrations of minorities in neighborhoods or in schools, and "desegregation" is commonly used to mean "racial balance." The change in meaning over a 25-year period has been of a qualitative nature with implications for policy. The policy implicit in these definitions is one of dispersion of racial minorities among the white majority in order to achieve desegregation, as it is presently defined.

What we must be concerned about in understanding the gradual redefinition of these terms is that the semantic discussion is merely the surface of larger issues. Beneath the surface are debates about how Blacks ought to fit into American society; how to make amends for the injustices of the past; how various minorities have achieved success in American society; how Blacks are similar to or different from other minorities; and what role the school plays in promoting the successful functioning of individuals and groups and in affecting the nature of community in modern America. We cannot understand the current arguments about the meaning of desegregation without directly considering these issues, examining their historical antecedents, their intellectual bases, and the choices implied for the future.

*   *   *

In the nineteenth century, one of the most fertile fields for speculation was, as it was then described, "the Negro question." What was to be done about the Negro? Here in these United States were millions of Black people, brought to these shores in chains, held in bondage, and kept in a state of ignorance. Numerous books and articles were written about "the Negro problem" or "the Negro question," and various proposals were advanced. What the problem was depended on the viewer's perspective. From a modern perspective, the problem was that white Americans tolerated human slavery and treated Blacks—slave and free—in ways that contradicted the expressed ideals of the nation. But to most white observers of the time, the problem was that Blacks were different, so different that there could ultimately be no place in this country for them. This view, which had broad currency, stimulated a number of predictions about the destiny of the Blacks. One of the most popular of these was the idea of colonization, either in Africa or some other warm climate. Advocates of colonization had many different motivations. Some felt that white prejudice against people of color was so intense that the departure of the latter from American shores was best for the sake of both. Thomas Jefferson repeatedly expressed the fear that Blacks would rebel against their masters or that deep-rooted prejudice would lead to a disastrous race war after emancipation. Some colonizers were convinced of the essential inferiority of Black people; others predicted that free Blacks, because of white prejudice, were bound to become a dangerous and degraded class. The supporters of the colonization movement saw it as an effective way to encourage gradual, voluntary manumission of slaves. While some colonizers truly believed in the equality of Blacks, their cause was a capitulation to white prejudice. As an answer to the Negro question, it promised a racially homogeneous America, an all-white nation freed of the Negro problem.[1]

In the early 1830s, the star of the colonization movement began to fade when the cause was vehemently denounced by William Lloyd Garrison as a plot to bolster the institution of slavery by eliminating free Blacks from the South. The abolitionists were not primarily concerned with whether the Black was assimilable, but with the very existence of slavery as an immoral institution that crushed human potential and violated American and Christian ideals.

Yet even among the critics of slavery, there were different understandings of what would happen to Black people after slavery ended. Some abolitionists were, in George M. Frederickson's term, "romantic racialists," who accepted the verdict of the crude social theorists of the day that the races were essentially different, each possessing special characteristics of mind and heart. Even in their defenses of Blacks and their attacks against slavery, the romantic racialists succumbed to the fallacy of ascribing different human natures to different races. In the racial stereotyping that was popular at mid-century, the Anglo-Saxon was a conqueror, a man of enterprise and intellect, a restless and hardy pioneer, and America was assuredly an Anglo-Saxon country. Romantic racialists, instead of rejecting the stereotypes altogether, claimed that the stereotypical Negro had much to offer the tough, insensitive, domineering Anglo-Saxon. The Negroes, said the romantic racialists, were a docile, gentle, emotional, and affectionate people; so simple and childlike was the man of African descent, thought some, that he was potentially a better Christian than the haughty Anglo-Saxon. To the romantic racialist, the solution to the Negro problem was some form of amalgamation, either the physical absorption of the Black race into the white majority, or cultural amalgamation, in which the special gifts of the darker race would enrich and ennoble the national character. These kinds of views, while intended to be humanitarian, were condescending, paternalistic, and patronizing; at times, they veered dangerously close to the idea of black inferiority. "It was never suggested," writes Frederickson, "that whites become literally like the black stereotype and sacrifice their alleged superiority in intellect and energy." In the proposed process of amalgamation, whether physical or cultural, there was never any question which race would remain dominant and which would eventually be submerged. It is in such views as these that it becomes clear that the *answers* arrived at were wrong because the *questions* and the underlying *assumptions* were fundamentally wrong.[2]

White supremacists had no trouble contemplating the future of the dark-skinned race; they were convinced that Blacks were inferior and well-suited to remain in slavery. Indeed, they maintained that slavery was a benevolent system in that it protected the slaves from a worse fate, that is, regression into barbarism. The doctrine of white superiority was bolstered by the work of the leading social theorists, whose ersatz "evidence" often included Biblical references and whose theories amounted to a justification of racial subordination. Their main ideas, which received broad circulation, were that racial differences were permanent and inherent, that certain races were innately superior to others, and that racial hybrids were weak and sterile. All of their theories and cranial measurements and proofs boiled down to a single assumption: that race is a fixed determinant of human behavior and character.[3]

The popular racial theories of the day influenced the context within which opponents of slavery analyzed the prospects for the Negro. Some critics of slavery predicted that the Blacks, once emancipated, would inevitably migrate southward to the tropics, a climate congenial to their racial inheritance. Others, anticipating the Darwinian concept of the survival of the fittest, held that the inferior Black race would eventually die out in the competition with the white race. Not everyone was willing to wait until the brutal laws of nature took their course, and in the decade before the outbreak of the Civil War, the colonization idea regained adherents. In 1858, an effort was made in Congress to win federal support for American Negro colonies in Central America; even during the Civil War, President Lincoln negotiated with Panama and Haiti for colonies and endorsed a government-subsidized program of colonization. Virtually all who supported colonization implicitly conceded that the white and Black races would not be able to live together amicably as equals. All of these various proposed solutions to the Negro problem had one common denominator: the eventual disappearance of the Negro as a disturbing presence in the American body politic. Whether by dispersion, migration, amalgamation, exclusion, or extinction, the anticipated result was the whitening of America.[4]

But none of these alternatives satisfied the radical abolitionists, who rejected all the conventional assumptions, all the popular wisdom, about the nature of race. It was the view of the radical abolitionists that Black and white people were members of the same race, the human race, and that all were individuals of equal worth. The problem, as they saw it, was that Black people were denied, by slavery and other human institutions, the freedom to develop their potential to the fullest. While others analyzed the Negro problem as a question of what to do about these people who were so different, the radical abolitionists understood that these people, because of the color of their skin, were *treated* differently. Given this analysis, the problem was not what to do about the Negro, but how to change those laws, institutions, and attitudes that permitted Blacks to be treated as less than human and less than equal citizens.

At the close of the Civil War, these views were advanced in the Congress by radical Republicans, who sought to protect the newly freed slaves from those who would restore slavery under another guise. Even though Southern representatives were temporarily excluded from the Congress, there were still legislators who objected strenuously to civil rights bills and guarantees of equality; their argument, bluntly stated, was that this was "a white man's government." In the debates between the radical Republicans and their opposition, the question facing the nation was, again, what is to be done about the Negro. The answer of the radical Republicans was that the Negro should be guaranteed full citizenship and equality before the law, and that these guarantees should be backed up by the Constitution. To achieve these ends, the Republican-dominated Congress pushed through the Thirteenth, Fourteenth, and Fifteenth Amendments, as well as civil rights legislation. And the purpose of the sponsors was unmistakable: it was to bar henceforth any discrimination based on race or color. Senator Lot M. Morrill of Maine acknowledged that the Congress was doing nothing less than reversing the Dred Scott decision and recognizing the Black man as a full-fledged citizen:

> If there is anything with which the American people are troubled, and if there is anything with which the American statesman is perplexed and vexed, it is to what to do with the negro [sic], how to define him, what he is in American law, and to what rights he is entitled. Hitherto we have said that he was nondescript in our statutes; he had no *status*; he was ubiquitous; he was both man and thing; he was three-fifths of a person for representation and he was a thing for commerce and for use. In the highest sense, then, in which any definition can ever be held, this bill is important as a definition. It defines him to be a man and only a man in American politics and in American law; it puts him on the plane of manhood; it brings him within the pale of the Constitution. That is all it does as a definition, and there it leaves him.[5]

The idea of wiping out all racial distinctions was a revolutionary idea, and it was an idea whose time had not yet come. Despite the passage of constitutional amendments guaranteeing equality, the doctrine of white supremacy in the South eventually outlasted efforts at Reconstruction. By the end of the nineteenth century, Black people were trapped in a state of peonage in the South, disenfranchised and powerless. The abandonment of the rights of Blacks is a familiar story, whose major features include the political deal struck to end Reconstruction, the activity of white terrorist organizations to intimidate Black voters, the Supreme Court's nullification of the Fourteenth Amendment as a shield against racially discriminatory laws, the spread of Jim Crow codes throughout the South, and the Court's 1896 endorsement of racial segregation. Once again, there was a "solution" to the Negro problem, and the solution now adopted was to exclude Blacks from the rights of citizenship.[6]

The doctrine of the *Plessy* v. *Ferguson* decision was the law of the land for nearly six decades; it symbolized the evisceration of the Fourteenth Amendment. But, echoing across the decades was a lone dissent from Justice John Marshall Harlan, a dissent which would serve as a benchmark for those who objected to policies of racial differentiation:

> . . . In respect of civil rights, common to all citizens, the Constitution of the United States does not, I think, permit any public authority to know the race of those entitled to be protected in the enjoyment of such rights. . . . in view of the Constitution, in the eye of the law, there is in this country no superior, dominant, ruling-class of citizens. There is no caste here. Our Constitution is color-blind, and neither knows nor tolerates classes among citizens. In respect of civil rights, all citizens are equal before the law,

When, in the early 1950s, NAACP lawyers decided that the time was right for a full-scale, frontal attack on the "separate-but-equal" doctrine, their briefs and arguments made numerous references to the principles enunciated by Justice Harlan. The chief argument in the *Brown* case was that "The Fourteenth Amendment precludes a state from imposing distinctions or classifications based upon race and color alone. The State of Kansas has no power thereunder to use race as a factor in affording educational opportunities to its citizens." The civil rights lawyers sought to establish that there was no difference between white and Black children and that state-imposed racial separation was arbitrary and injurious. The record built in Kansas was intended to show that black children in Topeka were assigned to public schools solely on the basis of their race, that these children had to travel past their neighborhood school in order to attend distant "colored" schools, that this arbitrary separation from others created within them a sense of stigma, and that long travel on school buses was detrimental to the healthy development of young children.[7]

The chief premise of the attack on segregation was that racial distinctions, for whatever reason, were unconstitutional and unreasonable. Robert Carter stated this succinctly:

> Now we rest our case on the question of the power of the state. We feel, one, that the state has no authority and no power to make any distinction or any classification among its citizenry based upon race and color alone. We think that this has been settled by the Supreme Court of the United States in a long line of cases which hold that in order for a classification to be constitutional it must be based on a real difference. . . . The Supreme Court has also held in a series of cases that race and ancestry and color are irrelevant differences and cannot form the basis for any legislative action.[8]

Within the appellants' brief to the Supreme Court, there was no question about the primacy of the principle of color-blindness. The brief maintained that "the Fourteenth Amendment compels the states to be color blind in exercising their power and authority. . . . this Court has uniformly ruled that the Fourteenth Amendment prohibits a state from using race or color as the determinant of the quantum, quality or type of education and the place at which education is to be afforded." The brief quoted Justice Harlan's famous dissent at length and stated simply: "That the Constitution is color blind is our dedicated belief."[9]

While the demand for color-blind application of the laws was the central thesis of the case against school segregation, a secondary theme was that Negro children were psychologically injured by being compelled to go to segregated schools. This argument went in two directions: One was the testimony that state-imposed social segregation was official sanction of the doctrine of Negro inferiority; the other was testimony that Negro children were injured by lack of contact with white children and thus deprived of experience with members of the majority group. In the first strand of social science testimony, the damage to the black child was caused by governmental coercion of attendance in a stigmatized school; in the second, the damage was caused by the absence of interracial contact. The first strand suggested a color-blind remedy, the second suggested an integration remedy.

This ambiguity within the *Brown* case can be traced throughout the record, from the original trial in Kansas to the final decision itself. In essence, the civil rights lawyers were simultaneously advocating both color-blind legal equality and color-conscious school integration. This ambiguity evolved during the following quarter century as an outright contradiction, since color-blind policies became, in many places, an obstacle to school integration. The possibility of a conflict between these two principles was not anticipated when the *Brown* case was argued before the Supreme Court. Responding to Justice Felix Frank-furter, Thurgood Marshall spelled out what he wanted: "The only thing that we ask for is that the state-imposed racial segregation be taken off. . . ." If school officials were enjoined from enforcing segregation, Marshall argued, "then I think whatever district lines they draw, if it can be shown that those lines are drawn on the basis of race or color, then I think they would violate the injunction. If the lines are drawn on a natural basis, without regard to race or color, then I think that nobody would have any complaint." Similarly, Spottswood Robinson, representing Black plaintiffs in Prince Edward County, replied to Chief Justice Fred Vinson: "Now, we submit that you cannot continue to discriminate against Negroes, or these Negro students; under the circumstances, what you do is, you simply make all the facilities in the county available to all the pupils, without restriction or assignment to particular schools on the basis of race."[10]

In light of this background, it is intriguing to realize that the most central precept of the case against segregation—Justice Harlan's principle of color-blindness—has since come under attack as a subterfuge for segregation. How is it that those who fought to remove from the states any power to make racial classifications now argue for school assignments based on race? These changes in meaning and purpose came about gradually but with significant effect.

There are several perspectives from which to assess these transformations of meaning. Clues can be found in, first, the political response of the South to the *Brown* decision; second, the attitudinal reaction of Northern liberals; third, the population movements of the past quarter century; and fourth, the implications of the common school ideal.

Of primary importance in shaping judicial remedies for racial segregation was the massive resistance by the Southern states, their concerted efforts to defy desegregation orders, and in some instances, their resolve to close public schools rather than permit white and Black children to attend the same schools. When open defiance failed, Southern districts shifted to evasive tactics to preserve dual school systems. By proposing "freedom of choice" in which community intimidation effectively maintained segregated schools, the Southern intransigents discredited the principle of free choice itself. In time, judicial orders began to counter strategies of duplicity and defiance by setting standards that, in some districts, required racial balancing as proof of compliance. Once the standard-setting began, the difference between *de jure* and *de facto* segregation became increasingly obscure.

In Northern cities, the *Brown* decision was early viewed as a declaration that predominantly Negro schools were segregated and inferior. It was often said that such a school could *never* be a good school. The liberal president of the New York City Board of Education told a Harlem audience in the fall of 1954 that there was no *intentional* segregation in New York, but that the schools their children attended were segregated nonetheless and were causing "a psychological scarring." The board publicly promised to reexamine the racial composition of its schools and to eliminate de facto segregation because racially homogeneous schools "damage the personality of minority group children," "decrease their motivation," and "impair their ability to learn." Given these assumptions, color-blind policy was tantamount to official toleration for schools that were segregated, inferior, and harmful to minority children.[11]

But what to do? White resistance to racial balancing was tenacious, and demonstrations of the low quality of Black schools simply confirmed white racist fears about Black neighborhoods, Black schools, and Black children. And the possibility of bringing about extensive integration through any color-blind redistricting diminished rapidly during the 1950s and 1960s, as whites moved out of cities and nonwhite minorities moved in. The spread of dense, racially homogeneous neighborhoods of Blacks and other nonwhite minorities meant that neighborhood districting or any other racially neutral scheme would not bring about the elimination of predominantly minority schools.

Yet another blow to the concept of color blindness was the fact that many, probably most, of those who advocated a color-blind approach wanted an integrated society as much as they wanted a society that was blind to color; there was certainly no desire on the part of racial liberals, black or white, to achieve judicial sanction for racially segregated neighborhoods or for racial discrimination that was disguised as something else. Thus, it was scarcely surprising that many of the same people who had fought most earnestly for the vindication of Justice Harlan's dissent soon began to search for policies that would bring about more interracial contact. Since there had been systematic exclusion of Blacks from participation in various careers, institutions, and centers of power, the transition from a policy of racial subordination to one of racial neutrality was fated to be an inadequate response; it simply could not guarantee Black entry into lily-white institutions. And yet, using race as the criterion by which to confer benefits or to impose restrictions has its inevitable cost. As the NAACP brief put it in 1953, "Any distinction based upon race was understood as constituting a badge of inferiority." And, as Thurgood Marshall argued, "racial distinctions in and of themselves are invidious."[12]

What ultimately undermined the full implementation of the color-blind principle was not just political, demographic, or ideological factors, but conflicting conceptions of the purpose of public schooling in America. Just as they do today, people in the 1950s had differing ideas about what the public schools were supposed to accomplish on behalf of society. Perhaps the most generally held conception was that of the public school as the common school, a school in which all sectors of the community learn together as equals and overcome differences in social origins; this common school, as it was projected by Horace Mann and other reformers of the 1840s and 1850s, was to be a great social equalizer, a pillar of democracy, and an agency of social assimilation. To those who saw the *Brown* decision within the context of the common school ideal, the implications of the decision ran counter to color-blind policy. For, if equality and democracy depend on a mixture of all races and classes in the same schools, then it becomes necessary to enumerate and sort and match children to achieve the right mixture.

Educators had long believed that a major purpose of the public school was to hasten the assimilation of diverse minorities to American culture. The public school had been generally charged with the responsibility of creating a unified American community by teaching a common culture and introducing children to the language, literature, history and hero-tales of the majority. One persistent problem was that the common culture was usually defined as white Protestant, Anglo-American culture and history, and the process of assimilation tended to mean giving up any culture or language that was different. Too often, "different" meant "inferior." For example, the mass arrival of millions of Italians and Jews at the end of the nineteenth century inspired fears that America was being overrun by inferior races and inferior cultures. One response was to cut off future immigration of these groups, another was to place new emphasis on the public school as an agency of Americanization and assimilation.

The common school, in its ideal form, has proved difficult to achieve, and it has historically worked best in areas that were largely white Protestant, where there was little dissonance between the culture of the school and the culture of the students. Part of the problem is that the ideal itself is a small-town ideology, which presents the vision of a school bringing together all the elements of an entire community under a common roof to live and learn together as equals. Transferred to cities, the same ideology has been realized only sporadically, since most big cities have within them islands of homogeneous ethnic groups. Thus, while a city like New York has had considerable mixture of children of different ethnicity in its schools, it has also had over the years many schools in which a single group predominated, be it Irish, Italian, Jewish, Black, or Hispanic.

Another impediment to the establishment of the common school ideal has been the fact that some minorities—ethnic, religious, or linguistic—did not want to be absorbed into the common culture. Some, like the Catholics, stayed out of the public schools and created their own schools, where they could protect their religious values against the implicit Protestantism of the public school. Others supplemented the public school education with their own cultural maintenance programs. To the extent that the common school was an agency of the melting pot, it has stimulated alternative traditions of schooling, which represent resistance to the assimilationist view of American citizenship. Such an impulse has generated support for the idea of the community school, that is, a public school that reflects and serves its immediate community. In minority communities, pressure has often been applied to public schools to make them more responsive to the surrounding community, in ways such as maintaining a library of Italian books or serving ethnic foods or teaching ethnic group history or offering bilingual instruction. There are many instances of public schools that made accommodations to those with different cultures; when the public schools fail to bend, groups with strong feelings about their religion, their heritage, or their language sometimes opt out and create nonpublic schools.

And yet, the important point to recognize is that assimilation of all of these groups into American society did take place, whether they were in the public schools or not. The public school was not alone in teaching immigrants the language of the land, its traditions, and its values; assimilation was also promoted by other agencies, such as the military, the press, political parties, labor unions, and the mass media. Eventually, as one historian points out, even "the educational agencies maintained by immigrant communities for the perpetuation of their own unique cultures were themselves transformed by Americanization. More and more, they became agencies not only for the transmission of immigrant culture to immigrant children but also for the mediation of American culture to the immigrant community."[13]

This legacy of conflicting interpretations of the role of the public school entered into the debate about the implications of the *Brown* decision. Those who believed that the public schools had brought about the social advance of European immigrants by speeding their assimilation expected them to do the same for Blacks. Those who saw the public school as an indispensable element in the successful functioning of the melting pot presumed that the school should play its customary role by contributing to the assimilation of Blacks.

It was not long before the conflict between the goals of color-blind policy and of assimilationist ideology became apparent. In the 1950s, social scientists who testified against segregation assembled evidence to show that racial differences were inconsequential and that children of different races had the same capacity to learn. Their emphasis on the basic irrelevance of skin color supported the lawyers' appeal against racial classifications.

But a decade later, the work of social scientists emphasized the importance of assimilation as a remedy for "the Negro problem," and the way that assimilation was conceptualized was closely related to prevailing ideas about Black culture. The literature of this period put heavy stress on cultural "deficiency" of blacks as a group and defined Blacks as an inferior caste that had been culturally and psychologically damaged by historic discrimination. Gunnar Myrdal had made this point in his classic *An American Dilemma* in 1944:

> *In practically all its divergences, American Negro culture is not something independent of general American culture. It is a distorted development, or a pathological condition, of the general American culture.* The instability of the Negro family, the inadequacy of educational facilities for Negroes, the emotionalism in the Negro church, the insufficiency and unwholesomeness of Negro recreational activity, the plethora of Negro sociable organizations, the narrowness of interests of the average Negro, the provincialism of his political speculation, the high Negro crime rate, the cultivation of the arts to the neglect of other fields, superstition, personality difficulties, and other characteristics are mainly forms of social pathology which, for the most part, are created by caste pressures.[11]

By the early 1960s, many social scientists had incorporated this perspective into their work, so that Black culture was viewed as a culture of poverty and the skin color of the Black person was itself a badge of caste; as one study of the personality of "the Negro child" argued, "The stigma of his caste membership is inescapable and insurmountable. It is inherent in his skin color, permanently ingrained in his body image.[15]

Most sociologists in the early 1960s seemed to agree that Blacks were trapped in an inferior caste status; that they could escape only by becoming integrated into a predominantly white setting; that Black culture was in various ways deficient for historical reasons; and that a predominantly Black school could never be a good school because it was predominantly Black. These ideas gave a cogency and moral force to the remedy of racial balancing. In accord with these assumptions, integration leaders often said that "real" integration could take place only with a white majority. New York State was the first to write this perspective into its educational policy: in 1963, the State Commissioner of Education declared that any school in which the students were more than 50 percent Negro was racially imbalanced and therefore incapable of providing equal educational opportunity. In effect, once a school passed the 50 percent mark, the predominance of nonwhites gave the school a label of "inferior." By April 1965, the Massachusetts Advisory Committee on Racial Imbalance and Education issued a similar policy statement, and one of the reasons they gave for eliminating racial imbalance was forthrightly based on the view that Blacks are a caste, not an ethnic group, and as such, have no culture to preserve. This is how they explained the difference between Blacks and European immigrant groups:

> History teaches us clearly why the Negro has not achieved equality in America as have the Irish, the Italians, the Jews. Only Africans, among all groups, were deprived of their cultural heritage. Only they were legally forbidden to marry. Only their children were taken from their parents to be bought and sold. The other groups, possessing a cultural heritage of their own, wanted to preserve it. For them, separation often meant protection; for Negroes it signified oppression.[16]

Meanwhile, among historians, a great debate has occurred about the Black experience in America. Histories by Stanley Elkins and Kenneth Stampp, both published in the late 1950s, argued that American slavery brutalized Blacks and damaged their personalities and cultural identity. More recently, histories by Eugene Genovese (1974), Herbert Gutman (1976), and Thomas Webber (1978) maintain that the Black family and Black culture were far stronger even under the constraints of slavery than earlier historians realized; their works make the case that Blacks created and sustained a viable culture, with its own values, traditions, social forms, and strengths. Each of these historical accounts treats a different facet of the Black historical experience, and the later works add an enriching dimension to the earlier focus on the victimization of Blacks.[17]

The emphasis in the earlier histories on the damage done to the culture and personality was an appropriate backdrop to the sociology of the 1960s, which analyzed Blacks as a caste group seeking to escape the stigma of their group identity through assimilation. This was yet another answer to the age-old question of what to do about "the Negro problem." There is a long-standing tradition in our historiography and sociology which holds that extensive assimilation of minorities into "the melting pot" is inevitable and desirable; it is only in the past fifteen years that Americans have begun to admit the possibility that members of minority groups can be different and part of the mainstream at the same time. While it has been widely noted that white ethnicity has persisted as a strong source of self-identity, despite the lures of the melting pot, social scientists have generally rejected the possibility that

Black culture might serve as a positive source of identity. Writing in 1964, one social psychologist countered white fears of racial miscegenation with the following argument:

> Curt Stern has demonstrated that if panmixis—completely random mating with no regard to racial differences—were to take place in the United States, the darker skin shades of Negroes would be virtually eliminated, but there would be little noticeable effect on the skin color of Caucasians. In other words, the Negro one-tenth of the nation would be 'inundated by a white sea' in respect to skin color.

The author then quotes Curt Stern, with a prediction that echoes nineteenth century ideas:

> When complete fusion has occurred, there will probably be no more than a few thousand black people in each generation in the entire country, and these are likely to have straight hair, narrow noses and thin lips. I suppose that if some person now living could return at that distant time, he would ask in wonder, 'What became of the Negro?'[18]

This, of course, is a statement of the melting pot ideology, which in its most ideal pronouncements prophesied a time when all Americans would blend together to form a new race, a new religion, and a new culture. What critics of the melting pot ideology argue is that many people are content to retain their culture, their noses, their lips, and their hair, so long as they can live in a society in which there are no restrictions placed on them for being different.

*   *   *

In assessing the meaning of the *Brown* decision today, we must recognize that it deals not just with the question of access to schools, but with the question of how to define Black people, and what part Blacks should play in defining their own purposes. If Blacks are seen as a caste group that has been deprived of its culture and its history, then one set of remedies seems appropriate; if seen as a self-conscious group with a viable culture, then other remedies might be in order. But whichever perspective prevails, the role of government must be to provide Blacks with the opportunity and the means to make choices for themselves, because it was precisely this power to make decisions that was denied to Blacks in the past.

So, the issues which policymakers must settle are complex. What should be common about the public schools? What should all Americans share in order to be fully American? How much difference is tolerable from one group to the next? How much difference is desirable in order to maintain a healthy diversity among our people? In seeking answers to these questions, we also confront the meaning of community in modern America. While it is a commonplace to say that the school should be closely related to the community, we should bear in mind that each of us is a member of many communities, because each of us has different interests and commitments. Person X is a member of a family, a neighborhood, a race, a religion, a regional community, a city, perhaps a nationality group, an occupation, a labor union, a political party, a sports group, a hobby club, a social group; some of these circles will overlap, others will not. The point is that none of us is one-dimensional, none of us is only a member of a racial group and nothing else. The more one participates in a variety of communities, the more democratic one's sense of community becomes. We tend to give conflicting signals to the school by asking both that it reinforce the values of a particular community and that it enable each individual to come into contact with a broader environment beyond his or her own group. The resolution of this seeming contradiction is to be found in the school's relationship to other educating agencies, some of which (like the family and church) teach the particular culture far better than the school, others of which (like the mass media and the political system) teach the universal far better than the school. Seen in this light, the school is the transitional agency between the particular and the universal. The problem is e pluribus unum, "out of many, one," and the question is a persistent American conflict between the legitimate demands of the many and the legitimate requirements of the society as a whole.

What, then, should desegregation mean today? Certainly, it should mean the removal of all barriers based on race, but it should not mean the dismantling of autonomous Black institutions, like the Black press, Black political organizations, Black churches, and Black communal societies. It should mean a heightened consciousness of the value of interracial contact in every sphere of activity, but it should not mean that a stigma must be attached to any activities pursued by Blacks without the participation of non-blacks. It should certainly mean participation by Blacks at every level of our political and economic structures, and it should therefore mean continued effort to increase the level of Black educational attainment and Black occupational achievement until racial differences are insignificant. In light of the demographic changes of the past quarter century, it should also mean the implementation of policies to provide and protect racially integrated neighborhoods inside and outside the cities.

This brief exploration of the interplay between past and present is intended as a reexamination of the intellectual bases of social policy. As such, it raises questions instead of providing answers. When we inquire into the meaning of segregation and desegregation, we find ourselves defining not just words or individual policies but the nature of the relationship of Black people to the rest of American society. And when we inquire whether Blacks are a caste, a race, an ethnic group, or some combination, the answer tends to imply some policy, since the definition contains certain assumptions about the value and extent of assimilation and about the strengths or weaknesses of Black culture. Questions necessarily arise as we explore definitions and policies: Is equality to be found only in the melting pot ideology? Are the cultural differences between Blacks and others a handicap or a source of diversity, to be eliminated or to be prized? What is the relation of the Black experience to that of other minority groups in America? Which values, which policies will bring us to a time in which people of all backgrounds accord each other the respect due every human being?

NOTES

1. Thomas Jefferson, "Notes on Virginia," *The Writings of Thomas Jefferson*, ed. Paul Leicester Ford, vol. 3 (New York, 1894), pp. 243–44.
2. George M. Fredrickson, *The Black Image in the White Mind: The Debate on Afro-American Character and Destiny, 1817–1914* (New York, 1971), p. 125; pp. 97–129.
3. For the racial theories of the period, see Thomas F. Gossett, *Race: The History of an Idea in America* (Dallas, 1963), and Fredrickson, op. cit.
4. Fredrickson, pp. 149–50.
5. *Great Debates in American History*, ed. Marion Mills Miller, vol. 7, "Civil Rights," pt. 1, p. 392.
6. C. Vann Woodward, *The Strange Career of Jim Crow* (New York, 1957); Kenneth Stampp, *The Era of Reconstruction, 1865–1877* (New York, 1966).
7. Brief for Appellants, Brown v. Board of Education of Topeka, United States Supreme Court, October Term, 1952, p. 5.
8. Appeal from the U.S. District Court for the District of Kansas, Transcript of Proceedings, Brown v. Board of Education of Topeka, 1952, p. 217.
9. Brief for Appellants, Brown v. Board of Education et al., October Term, 1953, pp. 22, 40–41, 65.
10. *Argument: The Oral Argument Before the Supreme Court in Brown v. Board of Education of Topeka, 1952–1955*, ed. Leon Friedman (New York, 1969), pp. 47–49, 71–72.
11. Diane Ravitch, *The Great School Wars: New York City, 1805–1973* (New York, 1974), pp. 252–53.
12. Brief for Appellants, Brown v. Board of Education et al., October Term, 1953, p. 34; *Argument*, Friedman, p. 45.

13. Lawrence A. Cremin, "Americanization: A Perspective," *UCLA Educator* 19, no. 1 (December 1976), p. 9.
14. Gunnar Myrdal, *An American Dilemma* (New York, 1944), pp. 928–29.
15. David P. Ausubel, "Ego Development Among Segregated Negro Children," *Mental Health and Segregation*, ed. Martin M. Crossack (New York, 1963), p. 37.
16. Report of the Advisory Committee on Racial Imbalance and Education, Commonwealth of Massachusetts, 1965, p. 3.
17. Stanley Elkins, *Slavery: A Problem in American Institutional and Intellectual Life* (Chicago, 1959); Kenneth M. Stampp, *The Peculiar Institution: Slavery in the Ante-Bellum South* (New York, 1956); Eugene D. Genovese, *Roll, Jordan, Roll: The World the Slaves Made* (New York, 1974); Herbert G. Gutman, *The Black Family in Slavery and Freedom, 1750–1925* (New York, 1976); Thomas L. Webber, *Deep Like the Rivers: Education in the Slave Quarter Community, 1831–1865* (New York, 1978).
18. Thomas F. Pettigrew, *A Profile on the Negro American* (Princeton, 1964), pp. 27–55, 62–63. For critiques of assimilation in American sociology and historiography, see Paul Metzger, "American Sociology and Black Assimilation: Conflicting Perspectives," *American Journal of Sociology* 76 (January, 1971); and Rudolph J. Vecoli, "Ethnicity: A Neglected Dimension of American History," *The State of American History*, ed. Herbert J. Bass (Chicago, 1970).

CHAPTER FOUR

How did segregation destroy the possibility that public schooling for blacks could encompass those prerequisites to effectiveness discussed by Sara Lightfoot and Diane Ravitch? Professor Charles Lawrence of the San Francisco School of Law contends that the purpose of segregation is not to separate the races, but to subordinate blacks in the society. The harm of school segregation—the inferior resources and the feelings of inferiority—is a manifestation of segregation that falls heavily on all blacks, whether or not they attend segregated schools. Likewise, all whites profit from policies of segregation that de-value the educational needs and worth of blacks. The only effective remedy for segregation, Lawrence maintains, is the affirmative eradication of segregation. But by requiring proof that school officials are responsible for segregation, and limiting relief to that harm attributable directly to school board policies, the Supreme Court has misunderstood segregation in order to justify remedies that bar only those blatant aspects of segregation no longer in fashion while ignoring policies, which, while "neutral" in terms, build on past precedents to continue black children in schools as inferior and ineffective as those they attended before *Brown* v. *Board of Education* became the law of the land.

"ONE MORE RIVER TO CROSS"—
Recognizing the Real Injury in *Brown:*
A Prerequisite to Shaping New Remedies

INTRODUCTION

It is time to evaluate the success of *Brown* v. *Board of Education* with the hindsight of a quarter century of history. We must decide, after almost three decades of life under the rule of law set forth in *Brown,* whether that decision should be tallied in the won or the loss column in black America's struggle for equality. But the theme of the Afro-American spiritual quoted in the title to this paper has a different thrust. Our enslaved forebears recognized that the white masters would not easily give up their preferred position, and that the struggle for freedom would not end quickly. There would be no final victory in their lifetimes. Each step forward was just that, a step. There would always be "one more river to cross."

If one views the *Brown* case narrowly, as a case intended to desegregate the nation's schools, history has proven it a clear failure. On the other hand, the success of *Brown* cannot be measured by reference to desegregation statistics alone, or even by looking only at how the schools are doing by our children. Even the immediate impact of *Brown* extended far beyond the schoolhouse. Judge Robert Carter noted that *Brown* fathered a social upheaval—the extent and consequences of which cannot even now be measured with certainty. There is little doubt that the psychological impact of *Brown* was the spark that ignited the spontaneous combustion of boycotts, sit-ins, voter-registration, marches, and political organizations that resulted in much significant change for blacks.

But the task should not be to add up the pros and cons of *Brown* and argue which list is longer or of greater significance. Any assessment of *Brown's* success should instead be an evaluation of where *Brown* has left us—an honest appraisal of where we stand so that we may better chart the course to our ultimate goal.

I have argued that the Supreme Court's reasoning in striking down an interdistrict desegregation order in Detroit was flawed in that it misunderstood the true nature of the institution of segregation.[1] The Court's failure to recognize and articulate the true nature of racial segregation was more the product of an intentional, knowledgeable decision than the result of any inability to comprehend. This intentional misunderstanding had its roots in *Brown,* and has judicial, political, and social attitudes which are crucial to Blacks today.

It is the thesis of this paper that the *Brown* decision fostered a way of thinking about segregation that has allowed both the judiciary and society at large to deny the reality of race in America, that the recognition of that reality is critical to the framing of any meaningful remedy—judicial or political—and that *Brown* may ultimately be labeled a success only insofar as we are able to make it stand for what it should have stood for in 1954.

I. HOW SEGREGATION FUNCTIONS

The full scope of the Constitutional injury inflicted by a segregated school system can only be understood if one understands how the institution of segregation functions. Three underlying characteristics of segregation are crucial to this understanding.

A. The first is that segregation's *only* purpose is to label or define blacks as inferior and thus exclude them from full and equal participation in society.
B. The second is that blacks are injured by the existence of the *system* or *institution* of segregation rather than by particular segregating acts.
C. The third is that the institution of segregation is *organic* and *self-perpetuating*. Once established it will not be eliminated by mere removal of public sanction but must be affirmatively destroyed.

A.   Segregation's Only Purpose Is to Stigmatize and Subordinate

That the purpose of the institution of segregation has always been to stigmatize and subordinate rather than to simply separate is perhaps best demonstrated by the fact that whites in the antebellum South had no aversion to commingling with blacks so long as the institution of slavery made their superior status clear. It was only with the demise of slavery that segregation became necessary. C. Vann Woodward has noted the virtual absence of segregation in the South during slavery.[2] Although historians differ in their views of when segregation became firmly established as an institution,[3] they are in full agreement in their description of the institution as an instrument of subordination which used a strict and rigid caste system to clearly define and limit the social, political, and economic mobility of blacks. Woodward has called "Jim Crow" laws the "public symbols and constant reminders" of the inferior position of blacks.[4]

Professor Charles Black has noted that the significance of segregation was best understood by looking at what it meant to the people who imposed it and to those who were subjected to it. He pointed out that it was actionable defamation in the South to call a white man a Negro, that placing of a white person in a Negro railroad car was actionable humiliation, and that a small portion of Negro blood put one in the inferior race for segregation purposes.[5]

In short, segregation American-style, like South African apartheid, has only one purpose: to create and maintain a permanent lower class or subcaste defined as race. Blacks are kept separate from whites not because it promotes efficiency in record keeping, or because their proximity produces toxic fumes that are harmful to the environment. They are kept separate because the separation labels or classifies blacks as inferior beings. Segregation violates the equal protection clause of the fourteenth amendment not because there is no rational relationship between the classification and the purpose—it is a supremely rational system—but because its purpose is illegitimate.

The holding in *Brown* that racially separate educational facilities are inherently unequal would make most sense if it were simply a recognition of the fact that segregation's purpose is invidious discrimination and that therefore it violates the equal protection clause by definition. But the Supreme Court avoided any recognition or articulation of this simple fact. Instead, the Warren Court based its holding on what it referred to as "intangible considerations." The Court said: "to *separate* [negro children] from others of similar age and qualifications solely because of their race generates a *feeling* of inferiority as to their status in the community in ways unlikely ever to be undone."[6]

The Court then went on to quote the federal district court in Kansas that found "a sense of inferiority" engendered by segregated schools "has a tendency to [retard] the educational and mental development of negro children."[7]

Instead of taking judicial cognizance of the fact that the manifest purpose of segregation was to designate blacks as inferior, holding such a purpose constitutionally impermissible, the Court chose to focus upon the *effect* of school segregation. Chief Justice Warren began the crucial portion of his opinion by describing the importance of education in achieving political equality. He then proceeded to cite evidence presented to the court by social scientists indicating that the effect of school segregation on black children was to generate "a feeling of inferiority" that in turn affects the motivation and ability of these children to learn. In short, segregation violated the equal protection clause because of its empirically demonstrated discriminatory *effect* on the educational opportunity afforded blacks.

Considerable controversy surrounded the original social science evidence that formed the basis of the court's "empirical" finding that segregation harmed black children, and the debate over whether placing black children in the same classes with white children in any way benefits them has been equally stormy.[8] If we think of the separation of black children from white as the sole source of the harm, the quarrel over whether their commingling helps remedy the harm seems important. But, because the mere physical separation of black children from white children was never the source of the harm, it makes little sense to look only at their physical integration for the cure. Once it is understood that the injury results from the existence of the label of inferiority, it becomes clear that the cure must involve the removal of that label. The mere placement of black and white children in the same school does not remove the brand imprinted by years of segregation.

By focusing on the effect of school segregation rather than its purpose the Warren Court confused the issue and led us to look to *separation* as the sole source of black children's feelings of inferiority rather than at the larger institution of which segregated schools were only a small part. This confusion has limited us both in proving injury and in our search for appropriate remedies.

B. *Black Children are Injured by the Existence of a System of Segregation, not Merely by Particular Acts That Result in the Segregation of Schools*

A second and related aspect of the court's misunderstanding of segregation is demonstrated by the court's adoption of the requirement that evidence of *particular* segregating acts by a *school district* exist before a federal judge may order relief against that school district. In *Keyes* v. *School District No. 1* the court found that there must be evidence that the racial imbalance in the *schools* was brought about by discriminatory actions of state authorities.[9]

Because segregation's purpose and function is to define or classify blacks as inferior, the injury that it inflicts is systemic rather than particular. Black school children are not injured as much by a school board's placement of them in a school different from that in which it has placed white school children, so much as by the reality that the school exists within a larger system that defines it as the inferior school and its pupils as inferior persons.

Many black schools that existed within the segregated school systems of the South were in fact superior to their white counterparts.[10] It is ironic that most of these schools achieved their excellence as a direct result of the discrimination inherent in a segregated society, in that the best black professionals were forced into teaching by their virtual exclusion from other fields. The existence of such schools violated the constitutional rights of children attending them, not because a school board or state legislature had taken steps to see that white children did not attend them, and certainly not because of the relative quality of education they provided, but because they were pieces of a larger puzzle, which, when fitted together, plainly spelled out the words, "If you're black, get back."

Once it is understood that segregation functions as a systemic labeling device, it should be clear that *any* state action that results in the maintenance of the segregated system is a direct and proximate cause of the injuries suffered by black children in segregated schools and is in violation of the equal protection clause of the fourteenth amendment. Evidence of such action would, of course, not be limited to acts directly resulting in one-race schools. Segregated housing and zoning practices are equally effective means of labeling blacks as inferior. If the state discriminates by continuing to participate in labeling blacks "not fit to live with," it is surely beside the point that it is not an active participant in particular acts labeling Blacks "not fit to go to school with."

Likewise, the scope of the injury cannot be defined by the boundaries of the school district that places black children in separate schools. State sanction of purposeful segregation that declares black children inferior in one district operates to stigmatize black children throughout the state. Black children in San Francisco do not escape the stigma when the state calls blacks in Los Angeles inferior. Nor is the scope of this injury limited to black children's relationship with the schools. The defamation reaches to the limits of its publication. It extends at least to the borders of the state and affects those children's relationships with landlords, neighbors, and future employers as well as classmates and teachers.

C.   Segregation is Self-Perpetuating: Once Established, It Will Not Disappear of Its Own Accord, and Its Elimination Requires Affirmative Action by the State

The Court's misunderstanding of the nature of segregation is perhaps best demonstrated by its failure to apply a consistent constitutional standard to Southern (de jure) and Northern (so-called de facto) varieties of segregation. Since de jure, as compared to de facto segregation, is found to arise by virtue of intentional acts of the state, this distinction is at bottom a state-action question. Although it is admitted that all segregation may result in injury to black children, the factual question that must be resolved by the court is whether the state can be held responsible. In states that had laws or explicit policies mandating segregation at the time of *Brown*, the answer was clear: this was de jure segregation and clearly unconstitutional under *Brown*.[11]

In 1973, the Supreme Court found that de jure segregation may also exist in the Northern and Western states where school segregation was not mandated by law in 1954. There is, however, an important difference, relating to the evidentiary burdens, between the Court's approach to establishing the presence of de jure segregation in the North and its approach to the same problem in the South.[12] In the North the burden is on the plaintiff to demonstrate the state's direct and causal involvement in the segregation of schools, while in the South the Court had held that the burden is on the defendant school district to demonstrate that it had acted affirmatively and successfully to dismantle a previously existing segregated school system.

In *Green* v. *County School Board*,[13] the defendant Virginia school district asserted the constitutionality of its "freedom-of-choice" plan (a plan whereby parents were nominally free to choose their children's school), by arguing that it was no longer directly involved in maintaining or perpetuating a segregated school system. The Court unequivocally rejected that argument and held that the school district had an affirmative duty to convert to a unitary system:

> In the context of the state-imposed segregated pattern of long standing, the fact that in 1965 the Board opened the doors of the former 'white' school to Negro children and of the 'Negro' school to white children merely begins, not ends, our inquiry whether the Board has taken steps adequate to abolish its dual, segregated system.[14]

Although the rejection of "freedom-of-choice" in *Green* appears to have been brought on by the Supreme Court's loss of patience with various Southern schemes designed to resist school desegregation, the Court indicated that the affirmative duty requirement grew directly out of the second *Brown* decision, *Brown II*, where the Supreme Court set forth broad desegregation guidelines for the implementation of *Brown* (I).

In *Green* the Court characterized *Brown II* as, "a call for the dismantling of well-entrenched dual systems." But the Court went on to indicate that it was limiting the affirmative duty requirement to those school systems that were segregated by operation of law in 1954 when *Brown* was decided. However, the rationale for the exemption of Northern districts from this requirement has never been made clear. Dual systems in Northern school districts have proven to be more firmly entrenched than those in the South. The argument that in the North there is no evidence of recent governmental participation in acts directly resulting in the segregation of schools was the argument advanced by the New Kent School Board in *Green* and rejected by the Court.

It could be argued that the Northern and Southern cases are distinguishable on the basis of state action; in the South, state action is present because state laws required the operation of dual school systems, while in the North, state action is absent because segregated schools occurred as the result of segregated housing patterns. This distinction, however, neglects the entire history of segregation in America.

Segregation is Northern, not Southern, in origin. The exclusion or segregation of blacks in public facilities was settled policy and reached considerable maturity in the North before moving South in full force.[15]

The official actions of Northern, Midwestern, and Western states played a predominant role in the entrenchment of segregation within their borders. The segregation of federal programs and facilities such as the armed forces and federal involvement in the establishment of segregated housing operated to injure blacks throughout the country and thus to abridge their rights under the Fifth Amendment. In view of the substantial state activity in the promulgation of segregation throughout the nation, the fact that the Northern states ceased official enforcement of segregated school systems prior to 1954, while the Southern states continued to do so officially, does not appear to be an adequate rationale for exempting Northern states from the mandate of *Brown*, as further elucidated by *Green*. Thus, the Supreme Court's distinction between Northern and Southern cases of desegregation is not really a matter of state action at all: it is simply a matter of timing.

Although the Supreme Court holdings dictate a chronological distinction between pre- and post-1954 legislation, the Court's reasoning in *Green* would appear to counsel the contrary conclusion; that the cases be treated on the basis of their facts and not be categorized by region or date. *Green* stands for the proposition that where a system of segregation remains firmly entrenched, the state must do more than cease and desist from further official support of the system; it must act affirmatively to disestablish that system. Once it is understood that segregation achieves its purpose by labeling blacks as inferior, it becomes clear that segregation is firmly entrenched when the label of inferiority is reflected in societal attitudes; moreover, once the label is firmly affixed, it will not be removed or alleviated by a mere discontinuance of official name-calling. This understanding applies to all instances of segregation and knows no geographic distinctions.

Gunnar Myrdal, in his monumental study *An American Dilemma,* identified the circular self-perpetuating nature of racial prejudice and discrimination as the principle of "cumulative causation." Once blacks are labeled as inferior, they are denied access to equal societal opportunities. The resulting inadequate educational preparation, poverty of cultural backgrounds, and lack of experience constitute real limitations on their ability to contribute to society, and the prophecy of their inferiority is fulfilled.[16]

The state has then acted to establish a self-perpetuating institution. Because there has been no affirmative action by the state to disestablish the institution, it remains intact. The segregated systems of the North and West are not *"de facto."* They have not occurred in the absence of official action. Rather, they are creatures of the state, and the affirmative duty to destroy them that was imposed on the New Kent School District in *Green* should be universally applicable.

Once the state has effectively institutionalized racial segregation as a labeling device, only minimal maintenance is required. Once the system is established, any attempt to distinguish "active" governmental involvement in racial segregation from "passive" or "neutral" tolerance of private segregation is illusory. Present passivity is merely a continuation of past action.

II. WHERE DO WE PROCEED FROM HERE?

Where does this analysis of what the Court has chosen to ignore about segregation leave us with respect to our initial query concerning whether we have won or lost *Brown* and where we must proceed from here? The Court's refusal to recognize and articulate the real nature of segregation in *Brown* and its progeny has fostered an attitude and approach to the elimination of segregation that necessarily be unsuccessful.

In the *Milliken* case, the Court's intentional misunderstanding of the institution of segregation allowed a rather facile rationale for the Court's no doubt politically motivated decision to keep black children out of Detroit's suburbs.[17] Well-established equitable principles require that the scope of the remedy not extend beyond the scope of the injury, said Chief Justice Burger for the Court's majority. Because the only injury he recognized was that created by official school board action separating black children from white children, Burger only found constitutional violations within the city of Detroit and, therefore, limited the remedy to that geographic location. Suburban districts had never separated black children from white for the simple reason that they had no black children to segregate. But surely the involvement of the public representatives of suburban citizens in maintaining the institution of segregation in housing, employment, banking and insurance practices, not to mention the state legislature's complicity in segregating Detroit's schools, did as much to stigmatize Detroit's black children and deny them access to full participation in society as did their separation from white children in the Detroit schools. Furthermore, there is no evidence that the state of Michigan, which required school segregation in 1845, has ever fulfilled the affirmative disestablishment requirement of *Green.*

A proper understanding of segregation would make clear the existence of injury beyond the Detroit School District line and the legality of the interdistrict remedy. But the failure of the courts to acknowledge the true nature and scope of the harm that segregation inflicts upon blacks has affected the progress of blacks in ways that go far beyond the issue of the legality or propriety of interdistrict busing orders.

A.   We must Devise and Demand Remedies That Go beyond Mere Pupil Placement

Our fixation on the question of the propriety and efficacy of the remedy of busing and racial balance plans stems in large part from our tacit acceptance of the Court's rather narrow definition of the injury of segregation as resulting from the separation of black children from white children and the fact that alternative remedies have rarely been requested, much less granted. Courts generally redress the constitutional injury of school segregation with orders that are limited to the reassignment of pupils, teachers, and administrators. But few courts have recognized the ubiquitous nature of segregation's injury or acknowledged the interrelatedness of its various aspects. Following the rule that the remedy must match the injury, judges have ordered that schools be desegregated if there has been evidence of school segregation, that Blacks be given access to housing if there has been proof of discriminatory real estate practices, that Blacks be given jobs if there is sufficient evidence of discriminatory employment practices, and that states that have engaged in practices denying Blacks the vote cease and desist from engaging in those practices. But each and all of these practices operate to stigmatize blacks and impede their access to equal social/political/economic opportunity or power. They operate cumulatively as well as separately to do so.

This means that it is not only appropriate but necessary for courts to look beyond the school system both to determine whether black school children's constitutional right to equal education has been violated and in formulating remedies to address those violations.

If the state has been involved in denying black children's families access to suburban housing, those children have probably been denied rights guaranteed them under federal and state fair housing legislation and the Thirteenth Amendment. But they have also been labeled as inferior by the state, an act that violates their right to equal educational opportunity under the Fourteenth Amendment as defined by *Brown*. It would then be appropriate for a court, having made a finding of discrimination in housing, to include the school system in formulating its remedy. Likewise if a court has found a school district to be guilty of segregating its schools, the injury derives not simply from the racial separation of students and teachers but from all extant forms of segregation or racial discrimination in which the state has played a part. The removal of any of those sources of injury becomes an appropriate remedy.

The small cadre of lawyers who formulated and implemented the *Brown* strategy were well aware that the desegregation of schools would not be a panacea. Their ultimate goal was full political and civil equality for Blacks; they knew that this could not be achieved until the entire system of segregation had been destroyed. In a speech before the National Bar Association in 1935 Charles Houston said, "Equality of education is not enough. There can be no equality under a segregated system. The American negro is not a dominant minority; therefore he must fight for complete elimination of segregation as his ultimate goal."[18]

The NAACP began its attack on segregation by asking that the *Plessy* doctrine of "separate but equal" be enforced in Southern graduate schools because they knew compliance was impossible and that each small gain would help advance the next stage in the struggle to destroy the entire institution. And when they had reached the stage at which they were prepared to challenge the constitutionality of school segregation itself, they chose to challenge this single aspect of the institution not because they believed that school desegregation would bring Blacks equality by itself, but because this was the one aspect of segregation upon which they had made a record and they knew they'd be damn lucky to get the Court to buy even this small piece of the solution, much less the whole thing.

As the NAACP lawyers had suspected, the Court was not prepared to take on the entire system of segregation, holding only that "in the field of public education the doctrine of separate but equal has no place."[19] Of course, *Brown* was followed by a series of *per curiam* decisions by the Court summarily declaring segregation illegal in a variety of public facilities,[20] and the case is generally read as invalidating all forms of state-sanctioned segregation. But the Court has never followed its reasoning in *Brown* to its logical conclusion. If state-sanctioned segregation injures black children by stigmatizing them (or engendering feelings of inferiority) then they are deprived of an equal educational opportunity by segregation outside of, as well as within, the school systems. As has been noted earlier, it is the existence of the system or the combined effect of many separate laws and state-sanctioned acts that labels blacks inferior. The injury inflicted by a segregated school system is inseparable from the injury inflicted by segregated housing or public accommodations because each reinforces the other and because the removal of one will not heal the injury without the removal of the others.

I have pursued the foregoing analysis in order to show that judicial remedies that allow for simultaneous and coordinated attacks on the multifarious aspects of the institution of segregation are legally defensible. But more important, any remedy that does not take into account the systemic nature of the injury of segregation is bound to fail.

My own experience as the principal of a community school in the black Roxbury section of Boston did much to illuminate for me the fact that reforms in our schools would have little impact on the plight of blacks if they did not take place in conjunction with reform in other segments of our society.

The Highland Park Free School was a product of the Boston School Committee's early 1960s resistance to desegregation and refusal to recognize the demands of black parents for an end to the inferior schooling of their children. Voluntary plans under which some inner-city black children were bused to suburban school districts provided a solution for parents who felt the only politically feasible way to improve the education of their children, and gain access to the resources available to middle-class whites, was to be with them. Other parents felt that the answer was to seize control of the schools from those who would use them to destroy their children. In most cities, the community control movement centered on gaining control of the public schools. In Boston, it manifested itself in the establishment of three alternative independent schools of which Highland Park was one.

The immediate goal of Highland Park parents was to remove their children from the brutalization and neglect of a racist public system and provide them with a school where they could learn basic academic skills from people they could trust to care for them. But, like all parents, they viewed schooling as preparation for their children's future—an avenue towards meaningful participation in the larger society.

The parent's immediate goal was largely fulfilled. The school was successful in engendering strong positive self-images among both children and parents, in creating an atmosphere in which children enjoyed learning, in expanding the school's role into a concern for the whole child and that child's family, and even in increasing scores on standardized tests. But there was little we could do to realize the parents' more long-range dreams. Even if we controlled the school we controlled little else. This became apparent as we began to talk about where our students would go when they left Highland Park. What were we preparing our children for? Would there be places for them to use what we were teaching them as fulfilled productive members of society? The teaching staff—educated in black colleges, for the most part—provided our children with positive role models, and our presence no doubt motivated their learning. But most of us had been tokens in a white-dominated university system. It was unlikely that many of our students would become professionals. A parent might tell her child, "Study hard and you'll end up like Mr. Lawrence," but, even without a full political analysis of why, both the parent and child would know the odds against that eventuality were high.

Our school was full of bright and capable children who would one day make fine artists, technicians, teachers, mechanics, lawyers, musicians, and businessmen. But few of them would get the chance. There will be little access to these jobs because increasingly there are fewer jobs than people, and because blacks have no power or control over the institutions that provide access to what few jobs there are.

I remember when I was in seventh grade, my social studies

teacher, in an almost all-white suburban New York school, used to give the same speech every time he passed out grades. At great length he would reassure the class that everyone had some talent. It didn't matter that you were better at woodworking or auto mechanics than you were at social studies or math. There would be a productive, fulfilling, and paying place for you in society.

At a very different level, my first year civil procedure professor, J. Willie Moore, assured all of us that our upcoming first-year final exams would not be the end of the world, by telling us of a former student: Moore had twice flunked him in civil procedure, but he had become a senior partner of one of the most prestigious law firms in Washington, D.C. "At Yale," he reminded us, "the A students become law professors, the B students become judges, and the C students make the money."

The point is that both my seventh-grade teacher and my first-year law professor knew that there would be a place for their students because in the relevant communities involved, the same people who controlled the schools controlled the jobs for which the school was preparing its students.

The traditional role of all schooling throughout history has been to prepare young people for the roles they will assume in society. The Exeters, Andovers, and Grotons prepared C. Wright Mill's power elite. Traditional women's schools have prepared girls to become subservient homemakers, social workers, or teachers. Segregated schools, prepare black children for a segregated society that relegates them to marginal roles. To change the racial demography of the school system is not enough. To spend more money, or change the curriculum, or the composition of the school board will likewise prove insufficient. As long as opportunity in the larger society remains scarce, those who are already reaping the benefits of privilege will insure that their children are best prepared to assume similar positions. Black children will remain "less qualified" until we gain representative influence in both the institutions of preparation and the institutions for which they are being prepared.

In 1954 we believed that school integration would break down racist attitudes by bringing white and black children together. In the isolated instances where there has been real integration the most obvious manifestations of individual racist attitudes have been overcome. One need only look at Bear Bryant's Alabama football team to understand how quickly racial attitudes can change when important things like national championships and television contracts are at stake. But the adjustment in an isolated individual's attitudes about who he or she is willing to sit next to and play ball with has done little to adjust the relative economic opportunity or basic power relationships between Blacks and whites in America.

B.   We Must Continue to Demand that the Affirmative Disestablishment of the System of Segregation Be Recognized As a Constitutional Right

Perhaps the most detrimental effect of the court's refusal to acknowledge the true nature and scope of the institution of segregation has been the resulting failure of the judiciary, and ultimately the public at large, to recognize a constitutional right to the affirmative destruction of that institution.

In an amicus brief to the Supreme Court in the Bakke case, the Committee on Academic Nondiscrimination and Integrity, a group that describes itself as a "representative cross-section of concerned scholars and teachers," characterized the university's goal of remedying past discrimination against minorities in institutions other than the medical school and by society in general as "an excuse for imposing their quota." "Indeed," the committee argued, "in many cases, the ancestors of reverse discrimination's victims were not even in the United States at the time of the prior discrimination against blacks and other minorities which is used as the excuse for committing reverse discrimination today."[21]

These sentiments expressed, in varying degrees of sophistication, by the opponents of minority affirmative action programs are reflected in Supreme Court doctrine as well as in the attitudes of an increasingly less generous American public opinion. The refusal of white Americans to accept responsibility for the relative educational, economic, social, and political disadvantage of blacks is legally and intellectually justified by ignoring the continuing vitality of the Institution of Segregation and their own role in its maintenance. White Americans deny responsibility for the position of blacks by denying that they have created a system of oppression that will continue to exist and operate to their benefit until they have destroyed it.

If *Brown* v. *Board of Education* stands for the unconstitutionality of segregation, then the Fourteenth Amendment must guarantee blacks the right to be free from the continuing force and effect of that institution, or it guarantees nothing. If one understands both the systemic and the organic/self-perpetuating nature of the Institution of Segregation then the affirmative disestablishment requirement of the *Green* case must apply not merely to school segregation but to *all* segregated aspects of American society.

But the Supreme Court has refused to recognize that segregation will not die a natural death. Perhaps the most important doctrinal consequence of this fact is the intent requirement articulated in *Washington* v. *Davis*[22] and *Arlington Heights* v. *Metropolitan Housing Development Corporation.*[23] In *Davis* the court held that the discriminatory effect of an entry level employment test did not violate the equal protection clause of the Fourteenth Amendment unless the plaintiffs could prove that the test was adopted with discriminatory intent or purpose. "[A] purpose to discriminate must be present," said the Court. But if the Court had acknowledged the organic nature of segregation there would be no need to find *new* discriminatory intent. It would be enough that a segregated police department had once operated as part of a state-sanctioned system of segregation and that the under-representation of blacks in the present department was a remnant of that system. The burden would rest on the state to prove that they had effectively destroyed the Institution of Segregation ("Root and Branch"). If that proof were absent, any continuing discriminatory effect would be attributable to the initial invalid intent or purpose in the creation of the institution that had never been destroyed.

In *Green*, the Court did not require plaintiffs to prove intent to segregate in outlawing the school district's adoption freedom-of-choice plan that appeared neutral as to race. It was enough that the private choices of parents to send their children to segregated schools grew out of a climate created by state-sanctioned segregation and that the defendants knew they could count on such a result.

In *Washington* v. *Davis*, the fact that blacks did less well on a standardized test was a direct result of the fact that Washington, D.C., and environs had maintained a school system segregated by law until 1954 *(Bolling* v. *Sharp)*[24] and had perpetuated that segregated system by using an only slightly more sophisticated system of classroom segregation through tracking until 1967 *(Hobson* v. *Hansen).*[25] Now the District of Columbia Police Department was using a method of selecting its employees that measured not what kind of police officers the applicants would make but measured instead the proficiency of their verbal skills. Like the defendants in *Green*, the defendants in *Washington* v. *Davis* could count on the continuing effects of their never completely destroyed system of segregation to maintain their mostly white police department. There was no need to initiate new non-neutral acts.

Of course the practical impact of the Court's requirement that Blacks make out a prima facie case of a discriminatory purpose has been to completely disembowel the Fourteenth Amendment's equal protection clause. Gone are the days when defiant whites proudly proclaimed racist motivation or clumsily covered their tracks after the fact. It is easy enough to find a nondiscriminatory rationale, such as a desire to upgrade the verbal skills of policemen or a commitment to single family residential housing. The fact that employment requirements or zoning regulations are facially neutral means nothing when they are little more than a measure of the education and income disparities created by the segregated system, and therefore can be counted on to keep the system in good working order. It becomes difficult, if not impossible, to prove discriminatory motivation when many of the practices that perpetuated the Institution of Segregation have become so ingrained that even the practitioners no longer recognize their intent.

In short, the intent requirement ignores the continuing vitality of the Institution of Segregation and exempts the present benefactors of that system from any responsibility for its continuing effectiveness.

The hostile attitude of many whites toward affirmative action programs in employment and education is also rooted in their refusal to acknowledge that the present superior status of whites is a direct result of a still operative system of segregation. They argue that blacks should not be granted so-called "preferential" treatment at the expense of whites who have played no part in denying them their rights. But if the system of racial defamation and exclusion was designed to perpetuate itself, the right of blacks to equal protection must include the right to the active destruction of that system. And as long as the majority continues to allow that system to exist (certainly as long as they benefit by its effectiveness), they play an integral part in the denial of blacks' right to equal opportunity.

In its decision in the *Bakke* case, a majority of the Supreme Court once again indicated its unwillingness to face the realities of segregation in America and make the equal protection clause more than an empty promise for blacks. By holding that race-conscious affirmative action could not be justified by the goal of remedying past societal discrimination but instead required judicial, legislative, or administrative findings of *specific instances* of unconstitutional discrimination, Justice Powell again ignored black Americans' *right* to an end to the segregated system.

The intentional segregation of Los Angeles, Pasadena, San Jose, and San Francisco schools, not to mention the Dade County Florida school system that Bakke attended, had as its *purpose* not simply the separation of black children from white, but the competitive disadvantaging of black children.[26] The white school board that segregated Bakke from his classmates *intended* that Bakke come to the medical school application process with better traditional credentials. And the regular admissions committee that chose to continue to rely heavily on the MCAT did so with full knowledge that a largely segregated American school system would produce few blacks who performed well on this facially neutral test. The System of Segregation continues to function without falter. To require a "specific finding" of discrimination by the medical school literally added insult to injury.

It is interesting to note that the *Bakke* decision has been described as a victory for blacks. Or at least as a Solomonic decision that gave half a loaf to each side. While the result could certainly have been worse, at bottom, Justice Powell's decision said no more than that whites could take steps to desegregate professional schools if they wanted to.

The irony of the debate surrounding the *Bakke* case is that there has been such virulent opposition to the idea that a state might be *permitted* to consider race in remedying the injury of segregation. The fact that minorities have a constitutional right to such a remedy has been lost in the concern for white plaintiffs who argue that they are victimized by affirmative action. Lost in this debate over so-called preferential admissions is the fact that medical schools are still over 90 percent white, that 95 percent of law students are white, and that in virtually every desirable job category, minorities come nowhere near having representation approaching their numbers. Lost is the fact that the new reverse discrimination plaintiffs are claiming the right to continued operation of a system that places them in a preferential position.

As Justice Marshall said in his separate opinion in *Bakke,* "we have come full circle." Just as the *Civil Rights Cases*[27] and *Plessy* v. *Ferguson*[28] destroyed the movement toward equality begun with the adoption of the thirteenth and fourteenth amendments, the notion of "reverse discrimination" threatens to halt the movement launched by *Brown.*

Plessy v. *Ferguson,* the landmark case that declared American apartheid lawful, and *Board of Regents* v. *Bakke*[29] seem, on first glance, to stand for principles that are diametrically opposed. After all, the words of *Plessy*'s lone dissenter, Justice Harlan, "The Constitution is color blind," have become the rallying call for opponents of affirmative action. But the ultimate message in *Plessy* and *Bakke* is the same. In both cases blacks are told we have no right to an end to the institution of segregation, and in both cases we are told that this is so because the injury we claim is a figment of our imagination.

In *Plessy,* the Court said "we consider the underlying fallacy of the plaintiff's argument to consist in the assumption that the enforced separation of the two races stamps the colored race with a badge of inferiority. If this be so, it is not by reason of anything found in the act. But solely because the colored race chooses to put that construction upon it."[30] The *Bakke* version of accusing blacks of groundless paranoia is less obvious. The requirement that "specific instances" of discrimination be established before affirmative race-conscious relief is appropriate denies the continued existence and ubiquitous impact of the injury produced by segregation. We who have known the "pervasive racism of our society, of which Justice Marshall spoke, are told it is not there. The argument that the constitution must be color-blind asks us to believe that *society* is color-blind, that segregation has died a natural death, and that each individual's success or failure is based upon a meritocratic measure of his or her ability and skills.

This version of America is comforting to those who are presently in the best position to reap the benefits of privilege. But the mythology of meritocracy does not jibe with the realities of American life. The sharp racial differences in life expectancy, medical care, income, jobs, education, and political power are all a part of that reality. To look only to educational reform ignores the disparities that go beyond differences in schooling (the fact that white high school dropouts have lower unemployment rates than black young people with some college education, or that the economic gap between Blacks and whites is widening, despite growing numbers of Blacks in higher education). The real resistance to the true desegregation of society comes from a fear of competition in a society where opportunities are limited.

By noting that the acknowledgment of the nature and scope of the injury of segregation is a prerequisite to meaningful remedies, I do not intend to infer that it is a sufficient prerequisite. It will not be enough that we are more articulate and imaginative in our pleadings and prayers for relief. The oppressor's understanding of his oppression is limited by self-interest, and ultimately we must find ways to make our oppression operate against the self-interest of those in power.

It is nonetheless important that we keep these self-evident truths clear in our own minds. Too often we have been sidetracked in our struggle because we have lost sight of our goal, or accepted the oppressor's definitions, or mistaken the means for the ends. We still have at least "one more river to cross." And unless we begin by being clear about the direction of the far shore, the depth, speed of current, and the physical properties of the water, we will never reach the other side.

NOTES

1. Lawrence, *Segregation Misunderstood: The Milliken Decision Revisited*, 12 U.S.F. L. REV. 15 (1977).
2. C. VANN WOODWARD, THE STRANGE CAREER OF JIM CROW, 3d ed. (1974), p. 97.

3. For a catalogue of the views on the historical development of segregation, see J. WILLIAMSON, ORIGINS OF SEGREGATION (1968).

4. WOODWARD, JIM CROW, note 3, p. 7.

5. Black, *The Lawfulness of the Segregation Decisions*, 69 YALE L.J. 421 (1960).

6. Brown v. Board of Education, 347 U.S. 483, 494 (1954).

7. *Id.*

8. Much of the social science evidence was considered weak when *Brown* was decided. *See* Cahn, *Jurisprudence*, 30 N.Y.U. L. REV. 150, 158–61 (1955); van den Haag, *Social Science Testimony in the Desegregation Cases—A Reply to Professor Kenneth Clark*, 6 VILL. L. REV. 69 (1960).

9. 413 U.S. 189 (1973).

10. Dunbar High School, in Washington, D.C., exemplified such institutions. "In the period 1918–1923, Dunbar graduates earned 15 degrees from Ivy League colleagues and universities, and 10 degrees from Amherst, Williams, and Wesleyan." Sowell, *Black Excellence: The Case of Dunbar High School*, 35 PUB. INT. 3, 7 (1974).

11. *See, for example,* Swann v. Charlotte-Mecklenburg B. of Educ., 402 U.S. 1 (1971).

12. Keyes v. School Dist. No. 1, 413 U.S. 189 (1973). Northern and Western cases following *Keyes* have been based on the standard for determining liability set forth in that case. *See, for example,* Morgan v. Kerrigan, 509 F.2d 618 (1st Cir. 1975) (Boston).

13. 391 U.S. 430 (1968).

14. *Id.* at 437.

15. C. V. WOODWARD, JIM CROW, note 4, at 17.

16. G. MYRDAL, AN AMERICAN DILEMMA 75–76 (1944).

17. Lawrence, *supra* note 3.

18. Speech by Charles Houston, National Bar Association Convention, "Proposed Legal Attacks on Educational Discrimination," (Aug. 1, 1935), uncorrected typescript excerpted in McNeil, "Charles Hamilton Houston," 3 BLACK L.J. 123, 126 (1974).

19. 347 U.S. at 495.

20. *See, for example,* State Athletic Commission v. Dorsey, 359 U.S. 533 (1959) (involving athletic contents); New Orleans City Park Improvement Association v. Detiege, 358 U.S. 54 (1958) (involving public parks); Holmes v. City of Atlanta, 350 U.S. 879 (1955) (involving public golf courses); Mayor of Baltimore v. Dawson, 350 U.S. 877 (1955) (involving public beaches).

21. Amicus brief of the Committee on Academic Nondiscrimination and Integrity, Regents of Univ. of Calif., 438 U.S. 265 (1978).

22. 426 U.S. 229 (1976).

23. 429 U.S. 252 (1977).

24. 347 U.S. 497 (1954).

25. 269 F. Supp. 401 (D.D.C. 1967), *aff'd sub nom.* Smuck v. Hobson, 408 F.2d 175 (D.C. Cir. 1969).

26. *See* Crawford v. Bd. of Educ. of Los Angeles, 17 Cal. 3d 280 (1976); Pasadena City Bd. of Educ. v. Spangler 427 U.S. 424 (1976); Gibson v. Bd. of Public Instruction of Dade Co., 272 F.2d 763 (5th Cir. 1959).

27. 109 U.S. 3 (1883).
28. 163 U.S. 537 (1896).
29. 438 U.S. 265 (1978).
30. 163 U.S. at 551.

RACISM
IN
PERSPECTIVE

Alan David Freeman
The Protection of Class Structure

Derrick Bell
The Relationship to White Interests

CHAPTER FIVE

Even lawyers favoring the *Brown* decision but critical of its enforcement are not of one mind. Charles Lawrence urges a corrective for the faulty judicial reasoning that has undermined *Brown's* potential. Alan Freeman, professor of law at the University of Minnesota, is far less optimistic. In his view, the resolution of racial issues in America is a matter of perspective. Minorities, as victims of discrimination, view racism as a universal wrong inflicted on them as a group, and only a group remedy that actually eliminates discriminatory conditions can bring real relief. Whites, as perpetrators, see discrimination as wrongs done by individuals, and acknowledgment of that wrong, by a law or decision, plus the willingness to enforce it against proven wrongdoers, ends discrimination even if, in fact, the discriminatory conditions remain unchanged. The law, with few exceptions, has followed the perpetrator model in racial cases. It has adopted rationalizations regarding the nature of violation, the character of proof, and the limitations of remedy to discredit the victim perspective. Professor Freeman suggests the rejection of the victim perspective is necessary to protect the existing class structure from bearing the cost of formal equality with the threat to vested interests, and the exposure as myth of the ideology of equal opportunity.

ALAN DAVID FREEMAN

SCHOOL DESEGREGATION LAW
Promise, Contradiction, Rationalization

INTRODUCTION

Constitutional law, especially with respect to racial discrimination, serves as more than "just law." It has served to articulate the evolving statement of dominant moral consciousness (supposedly of "our society") about that subject. As such, the development of legal doctrine over time seems to implicate much more than the parochial concerns of legal technicians. Consider, for example, the furor over the *Bakke* case,[1] and the massive and ritualistic "looking to the Supreme Court" for the latest moral pronouncement on the subject of race. Against this background, I will discuss three major themes.

The first theme (or thesis—it's a little of each) is that antidiscrimination law as it has evolved since the *Brown* case[2] in 1954, up through the *Bakke* case in 1978, has served more to rationalize the continued presence of racial discrimination in our society than it has to solve the problem it ostensibly set out to solve, or to promote the human liberation one would have expected from such a body of law. I suggest that the doctrine can be described more convincingly in this fashion than in a more conventional positive, progressive, or reformist sense.

This paper is based on Professor Freeman's much longer project, the first part of which appears as *Legitimizing Racial Discrimination Through Antidiscrimination Law: A Critical Review of Supreme Court Doctrine*, 62 MINN. L. REV. 1049 (1978). A second part is currently in manuscript form and titled *Legitimizing Racial Discrimination Through Antidiscrimination Law (Part II): Race, Class, and Equality of Opportunity*. A version of that part was presented at the Second National Conference on Critical Legal Studies, held at Madison, Wisconsin, over the weekend of November 10–12, 1978.

The second theme has to do with the tension between the experiential uniqueness of racial discrimination and its remedial intractability as a separate phenomenon. There is no doubt that racial discrimination in American life and history has been a distinct form of oppression, something different from other relations of exploitation. Nevertheless, the history of antidiscrimination law suggests to me that no genuine liberation or genuine change in the conditions associated with the historical practice of racial discrimination can be accomplished without tackling the American class structure. For no matter how hard one tries to deal with the unique problem of race, deep structural obstacles make it difficult to proceed very much further than we have already.

The third theme, which is related to both of the first two but is more parochial (in that it's directed more at law professors), is that we are in the middle of a crisis of legal scholarship. How is one to talk about a body of legal doctrine such as the one I am describing today? Where are the reference points? What must be presupposed to gain the advantage of an easy scheme or frame of reference? There are many groping efforts going on, quests for new formalisms, toward shared values that can be hauled out as objective references against which to test and evaluate the outcomes of seeming conflicts. There is even the quest for the most rigid of neo-formalism represented by the "law and economics" movement, which may also be seen as politically reactionary. The problem is how to fill the intellectual vacuum.

What is the reference point when one looks at a body of legal doctrine and sees no objective referents? I have become more interested in questions of conflict, questions of struggle, and questions of voice. Who is speaking to whom, and in whose interests? The assertion of abstract universals leads me to wonder what actuality is being rationalized. What shared values are asserted? Whose values are they? In whose interests do they exist as values? What do they presuppose? What vision of the world is presupposed by the assertion of abstract ethical principle, and what's the relationship between that vision of the world and the one we live in? I tend to see the movement of legal doctrine as a continuing dialectic of struggle, characterized by value clashes that do not incorporate varying frames of reference and share no agreed-upon reference point. And the struggle seems to be an authentic one, with uncertain outcomes, and potentials for attaining results.

Despite the authenticity of the struggle as it happens, one begins to wonder after studying and reflecting on experiences like the civil rights struggle over the long period of time under review. Is there a metaphor in the experience of having rooted for the Red Sox in the middle of the summer? One knows that the Yankees are always going to win. They may not win every year, but they do always Win. But how does that knowledge relate to the consciousness of the fans and players during the season? You go to the field and think "today we can win, we can do it." How does that consciousness relate to the perception of long-run Yankee victory?

The task for scholarship becomes one of both preserving the authenticity of the struggle and finding a way to talk about structural constraints, without adopting simple reductionist approaches. I do not contend that one could have predicted the precise course of Supreme Court doctrine over the period since the *Brown* decision: I do suggest, however, that when one looks at the body of doctrine that emerged, one becomes suspicious. In whose interest did this really happen? Are there alternative formulations that might make more sense than one presupposing a model of gradual, reformist striving toward the utopian world of color blindness? If such formulations are available, let's begin to talk about them. Let's be bolder than timid in our willingness to make wild assertions as a beginning of conversation on a different level. It is to that enterprise that I dedicate the remainder of this paper.

I. VICTIM AND PERPETRATOR

The starting place for a discussion of racial discrimination would seem to be the concrete experience of a person who belongs to the group that has been discriminated against. What does it mean to such a person to be told that racial discrimination has now become illegal? The *Brown* case surely had to do with more than education. It was the official American statement that racial discrimination had become illegal (and immoral). The meaning of such a statement, to a black American in the fifties (or even now) must include an expectation that there will be, when the task is completed, some significant change in the conditions of life that one associates with the past practices of discrimination—segregated schools, lack of jobs, the worst jobs, lack of political power.

If making racial discrimination illegal is to make any sense, it must include some significant change in those conditions. Or, to the extent that such conditions persist well after the change in legality, they must become explicable not as the product of a society that has practiced racial oppression, but as consistent with the way the good society should work. For example, if, after the "elimination" of racial discrimination, substantially disproportionate numbers of black people still have the worst jobs, my reaction is that change has not occurred, discrimination has not been eliminated.

An alternative response, that one hears with increasing frequency today, is that jobs are maldistributed not because of the failure to eliminate racial discrimination, but because of insufficient merit, or lack of qualification. This quickly becomes what others have called the "blaming the victim" approach.[3] The idea is that if there's fault, it's the fault of the black people who have not made the best of the new era of nondiscrimination. But to make such a wild assertion seems to presuppose the world that has transcended racial discrimination is already functioning—that, for example, the myth of equality of opportunity is, in fact, a reality. My preference, faced with such a question, is to ask whether the myth isn't working. Perhaps we should presume the opposite way: When the very conditions that one used to associate with the most blatant forms of discrimination have not gone away, perhaps our "other institutions" are not yet the ones appropriate to future society; perhaps there is still something wrong with them.

Thus it seems to me that results are crucial. Instead, we have today a body of antidiscrimination law that makes results largely irrelevant. The moral consciousness reflected in that law has become indifferent, for example, to whether a "desegregated" school becomes one that is in fact integrated (I do not at the moment mean to imply anything about the educational efficacy issue, which I think raises separate questions). The same is true for educational admissions and for employment.

By making results irrelevant, the law ultimately fails to speak to the concrete perception I began with. I have called that concrete perception the victim perspective on racial discrimination. This approach illustrates my earlier point about legal scholarship that listens for different voices, or looks for different perspectives, instead of fruitlessly searching for an elusive unity. The core idea of the victim perspective is that doing something about the problem of racial discrimination necessarily means results.

Modern American law instead has adopted what I have called the perpetrator perspective. It is the stance of society as a whole (or pretends to be)—a third-party gaze looking down on the problem of discrimination. The perpetrator perspective doesn't care about results. Discrimination becomes the actions of individuals, the atomistic behavior of persons and institutions who have been abstracted out of actual society as part of the quest for villains. It is a notion of racial discrimination as something that is caused by individuals, or individual institutions, producing discrete results that can be identified as discrimination and thereafter neutralized. The emphasis is negative—on the behavior of the perpetrator and not the life situation of the victim. It requires great efforts to identify and catalogue perpetrators, to make sure that one has ascribed the correct evils to the correct perpetrator.

The perpetrator perspective, which is the principle model of contemporary antidiscrimination law, presupposes that apart from the misguided conduct of particular actors the rest of our society is working, that future society is otherwise here. All we need do is root out the villains. Having done so, we can say with confidence that it was all their *fault*. One aspect of the fault notion is very, very pernicious: those who are not, under current versions of the doctrine, labeled perpetrators, have every reason to believe in their own innocence. If you are not a perpetrator, you must be just an innocent societal bystander. And why, then, should you be called to account or implicated at all in the business of eradicating the past? You're not guilty. I believe that this aspect of the perpetrator perspective has a great deal to do with the psychic structure of the *Bakke* dispute.

While the perpetrator perspective captures the content of contemporary antidiscrimination law, it has not evolved neatly. The doctrinal evolution can best be described as having toyed with the victim perspective while retaining the form of the perpetrator perspective. That story begins with the *Brown* case.

II. THE DOCTRINAL EVOLUTION

Antidiscrimination law has passed through three eras of decision-making since the *Brown* case. The first era I call the "era of uncertainty," or, alternatively, the "jurisprudence of violations." It covers the period from 1954 to 1965, when the law was preoccupied with identifying violators and violations, with extending the scope of antidiscrimination law rather than remedying what had been deemed violations. While it is true that lower courts during that era began to struggle with questions of remedy, at the level of Supreme Court doctrine, answers remained uncertain.

The period from 1965 to 1974 I call the "era of contradiction," or the "jurisprudence of remedy." During that era, the Supreme Court adhered ostensibly to the perpetrator form, concerning itself with questions of fault and causation at a formal level, but regularly deviated from the substantive requirements of the form, in fact often contradicting itself. Thus the Court created the hope that it was, or seemed to be, incorporating the victim perspective in its decision-making, while steadfastly insisting that it was doing nothing of the kind.

The third era, which I call the "era of rationalization," or the "jurisprudence of cure," began for school desegregation law with the 1974 decision in *Milliken* v. *Bradley (Milliken I)*.[4] The Court reasserted the substantive primacy of the perpetrator perspective by pretending never to have strayed away from the results of several earlier cases. But I do not suggest a cyclical view. The Court did not start with one view, adopt a new one for a while, and then simply return to the earlier one. It is crucial to this evolution that the return to strict perpetrator form occurred after having passed through the interim period. For that interim enables the Court to say today that there has been a cure. Because of what happened in the interim, the Court can say today, for example, that Detroit's schools are desegregated. But that's the end of the story, and it is time to return to the beginning.

In the *Brown* case, there was no particular reason, as a matter of legal doctrine, to think about the victim-perpetrator dichotomy. At the same time, as I suggested earlier, the victim perspective was crucial to the concrete expectations reasonably arising in the people whose liberation was announced by the decision. But even as a matter of legal doctrine, there has been great debate about what the *Brown* decision "meant." In one sense, there is no issue, as Professor Charles Black made perfectly clear in the most sensible article ever entered in the "meaning of *Brown*" debate.[5] The *Brown* case was "about" white oppression of blacks. Segregation was illegal because of its role as part of that system of oppression. But that accurate statement does not resolve the victim-perpetrator issue, does not yield an appropriate abstract principle. It is an instance of method, of how to decide the meaning of a concrete historical event.

But the *Brown* case also produced doctrinal abstractions. In fact, one way of gauging the extent to which such abstractions respond to problems and needs other than the one to which they ostensibly respond is to look at the gap between such abstractions and the concrete historical actuality that generated them. The most significant such abstraction, one far removed from the white oppression of blacks actuality, is the theory of color blindness. But prior to the color-blindness view, the issue was asserted to be one of freedom of association. That view cannot be said to capture the "meaning" of *Brown*, at least by way of hindsight, but it was in many ways an accurate statement of what *Brown* meant for the moral consciousness of the fifties, for a world where, by and large, private discrimination (at least at the national level) was still regarded as ethically okay. Freedom of association is thus a way of rationalizing *Brown* for a world that hadn't yet, even as a matter of fashion, ruled out discrimination, but was beginning to do so. The principle may be regarded as an interim ideology, pending the change in public fashion that now includes such powerful superficial symbols as the black faces on the television ads.

Color blindness has remained an important component of the legal ideology of antidiscrimination. When I refer to the modern perpetrator perspective, I mean something more than color blindness, but the color-blind view exerts a continual pressure on the overall perpetrator view. The color-blind view seems to presuppose an abstract, ahistorical future world. The rules of color blindness are the ones that would be appropriate, and would hence be superfluous, in a society that has never known racial discrimination.

The color-blind theory arose in a concrete setting, in the famous Harlan dissent,[6] as an objection to segregation. The curious ideological phenomenon is that color blindness has become an abstraction that has taken on a life of its own, one that can turn around to disappoint the hopes of the very people on whose behalf it arose initially. Why should color blindness be an end in itself, a reference point against which to test questions of racial discrimination? It has become a way of abstracting the American black experience out of its own historical setting to the point where all ethnics become fungible under the pressure of color blindness. I don't think all ethnics are fungible; I think people have had very different experiences, and that the ideology of fungibility is part of the process of refusing to deal with the concreteness of black experience.

The color-blind approach maintains an insistent pressure on antidiscrimination law, because it is supposedly one of those "cherished" and "shared" values. Again, I ask: Whose values? In whose interest? pure form had left antidiscrimination law and been replaced with the greater sophistication of the perpetrator perspective. It has had a resurgence, however, with the fragile "majority" in the *Bakke* case.[7] Justice Powell, in his crucial opinion, seemingly relies on the most rigid rhetoric of color blindness, although in many ways undercutting himself with what must be interpreted as an implicit invitation to hypocritical practice.

Another view of *Brown* is the idea of equality of educational opportunity. I think that the notion of equality of opportunity is an accurate way of describing what the litigants in *Brown* had in mind. That view is somewhat ironic since the opinion has come to stand for both more and less than equality of educational opportunity—more to the extent it reached out to strike down other discriminatory practices, but much less to the extent there is no recognized right, no ethical claim for equality of resources or a substantively effective education as such. But even equality of educational opportunity was never an end in itself. It was, and is, a means toward dealing with the greater problem of liberation, toward reversing the conditions associated with the history of oppression. And equality of educational opportunity is a functional goal only if one presupposes a working system of equality of opportunity *in general,* operating in harmony with the educational system. What happens if one discards that presupposition, and questions the myth of equality of opportunity more directly?

From the victim perspective, equality of educational opportunity cannot be treated as an end in itself; it may be a means. The same is true for the vision of the integrated society. I think that for the most utopian interpreters of *Brown,* it was the beginning of the end of racial discrimination, an end that would be achieved when, by the year 2200, everyone had become a creamy shade of beige, and race had simply ceased to exist under the guiding hand of genetic entropy. Integration need not be an end in itself; however, it remains a powerful symbol of liberation. From the victim perspective, a choice of means other than integration may be no more than a choice of means, a strategic decision to seek the single end of liberation by another path; but apparent choice is too often a mask for imposition or rationalization, especially where the resultant conditions seem so identical to those that have for years been a symbolic measure of oppression. And the problem is underscored by the fact that the perpetrator ideology employed as part of the rationalizaton process seems to presuppose the achievement of an integrated society.

The *Brown* case simply set loose these various ideas and expectations, raising ambiguities to be resolved at a later time. On one occasion toward the end of the first era, however, the Court did have to confront the perpetrator-victim dichotomy. In a jury discrimination case, *Swain* v. *Alabama,*[8] the Court had to choose, and chose the perpetrator perspective, making it irrelevant whether any black people in fact served on the juries at issue. To back up its position, the Court invoked the language of color blindness, combining ethnic fungibility with the impropriety of claims to proportional representation.

During the second era, the era of contradiction, the Court had to contend with the perpetrator-victim issue. The major cases were *Green,*[9] *Monroe,*[10] *Swann,*[11] *Wright,*[12] and *Keyes.*[13] In each of these cases (except perhaps *Green,* which is more transitional and more easily reconciled with the perpetrator form), the Court adhered to the perpetrator form while incorporating the victim perspective, creating expectations that changes in conditions had become a matter of entitlement in antidiscrimination law. Here, I refer to motivations in decision-making similar to those Derrick Bell characterized as "antidefiance" decisions. My own, and very related, characterization, arises from three typical kinds of discrimination cases.

The three recurring case types led the Court almost by necessity, if it was to preserve any integrity in its doctrine, to incorporate the victim perspective. One version is the "infinite series" problem. A voting example is illustrative. Suppose a municipality has gerrymandered its districts so that the entire black population is in one district, and every other district is white, and you have evidence of purposeful discrimination. If you go to court and get the practice declared illegal, what's the remedy? Suppose the court simply issues an order to the municipality that says, "Stop doing that." And then a redistricting follows, with most of the black population still in the one district, and a handful of people shifted elsewhere. Assume there is no further evidence of "purposeful" discrimination. How do you know if the new scheme is a violation or not? If the degree of change from the initial scheme is slight, one is inclined to require further change. But how much? The problem is that remedying such a violation doesn't make much sense unless you incorporate some notion of racial proportionality. But that is a victim perspective notion.

And instead of going through a process of repetitive litigation that approaches a limit of proportionality, it may be easier and more convenient to insist on such a remedy at the outset. The Voting Rights Act exemplifies this problem and its solution, the actual infinite series litigation had taken place in the South over voter eligibility issues for years prior to the enactment of the statute. Focusing again on the hypothetical districting case, I suggest that once the notion of proportionality creeps in, there is created an expectation that if you prove a violation, you will get proportional representation. But simultaneously, it is difficult to relate the remedy of proportionality to the violation. All the violation demanded was a negation. And if there is a right to proportionality here, why not elsewhere? In fact, what does proof of the violation really have to do with the legitimacy of the claim of proportionality, unless, of course, one is already in future society? Thus, what was clearly a perpetrator perspective occasion for intervention leads almost unwittingly to the creation of a victim perspective expectation.

Another typical case is the "no result" problem. *Swann* is a good illustration. Here, the evil is embarrassment. *Brown* declared segregation illegal, but through its relegation of remedial issues to lower courts, chose to do nothing about the problem. While the Court waited, the world changed. Neighborhood patterns shifted; residential segregation increased. By the time the court returned to the original problem, to do nothing but outlaw segregation would amount to the embarrassing situation of having done nothing once again but make a statement. Even Justice Frankfurter had worried publicly during the oral argument in *Brown* that "nothing would be worse" than for the Court "to make an abstract declaration that segregation is bad and then have it evaded by tricks."[14]

But the Court could not go back in time. Thus it had to order a jurisdiction that would have had some racial balance in its schools had the Court insisted on immediate and massive enforcement of *Brown* to achieve that same racial balance fifteen years later, knowing, and simultaneously denying, that something had happened in the interim to frustrate all possibility of success in the original expected terms. By proceeding that way, the Court created the expectation and assumption that if the real relationship between the original violation and the current condition were actually that tenuous, it must be the current condition that is significant regardless of the original violation. From the victim perspective, the expectation becomes a change in conditions. The concrete expectation goes to results, while the Court indulges itself with verbal gimmickry to "show," through the use of self-contradictory presumptions, as in *Swann,* how the current conditions are related to the original violation. In *Keyes,* the Court used similar gimmicks; in *Wright,* the Court limited its concern to "effect." The net effect was the creation of perception, consistent with the victim perspective, that the problem was not just the old practice of segregation but the current pattern of racially concentrated schools. That perception gave rise to an expectation of entitlement, an affirmative right, to integrated schools (schools that are in fact integrated) for some period of time sufficient to make credible to the black people involved the claim that segregation had been outlawed.

A third type of case may be called the problem of the neutral practice, or the ostensibly neutral practice. Although the notion is directly applicable to school cases, and especially to zoning and districting for school attendance, the best illustration is an employment case— *Griggs* v. *Duke Power Co.*[15]—a case that I regard as the central case of the era of contradiction. *Griggs* was the only Supreme Court case that just about incorporated the victim perspective. Not surprisingly, it is one of the most currently repudiated cases, if one observes the efforts[16] being undertaken to narrow it, to stomp on it, to beat it to death, to avoid extending it to other areas. *Griggs* involved a neutral practice—testing—that was in its own narrow context probably being employed for the purpose of racially discriminating, given the sequence of events in that case. But there was no provable causal link between the substantive validity of the test itself (as opposed to the probably intent with which it was employed) and the employer's prior practice of blatant discrimination.

So here too the Court, in order to deal with what was basically a perpetrator perspective problem, went to the victim perspective by looking at the test itself rather than the prior practice of discrimination. The test was just a neutral practice that happened to fall with disproportionate severity on black persons required to take it. Under the perpetrator perspective, neutral practices are normally presumed to be the ones we would have in future society. The mere fact of a racially disproportionate result normally raises no issue, since there is no guilty perpetrator from that fact alone. Under the idea set loose by *Griggs*, however, ostensibly neutral practices had to justify themselves because of their ill results. And that added a new and dangerous notion—dangerous to the perpetrator perspective—that other neutral practices, regardless of their particular history of use, might similarly be called upon to justify themselves. And that notion suggested, consistent with the perpetrator perspective, that the concept of intent in antidiscrimination law had changed, that intent had more to do with continuing a course of conduct producing undesirable results than with why one engaged or continued the course of conduct. This amounts to incorporation of the victim perspective.

There was no reason to suppose at the time of *Griggs* that its notions would not be extended to all other areas of civil rights law, especially school desegregation law. Since *Swann, Wright*, and *Keyes* followed *Griggs*, one reads them strongly influenced by the assumption that the *Griggs* idea applies to the neutral practices in those cases as well, especially the practice of neighborhood school assignment. And all the while, the Court steadfastly adhered to the perpetrator perspective form. In *Swann*, the Court insisted on symmetry of remedy and violation, talked about causation and intent. In *Keyes*, at one and the same time the Court reminds us of the need to prove intentional discrimination and affirms a lower court that essentially found segregation on the basis of little else than result, using a tort standard of intent. One is left boggled, puzzled; the victim perspective has crept into the law.

And then came *Milliken* v. *Bradley (Milliken I)*[17] and the subsequent cases, with their rigid insistence on strict compliance with the perpetrator form. In *Milliken*, the neutral practice was jurisdictional districting, which the Court called local autonomy. And a version of local autonomy that includes not just the *idea* of local control but the *fact* of the particular districts involved is elevated by the Court to the status of a cherished, constitutional value. How does that compare with the opposite treatment of neighborhood school districts in the *Swann* case? Characteristic of the third era, the era of cure, the rationalization, is a strict and fastidious insistence on every aspect of the perpetrator perspective. The Court demands proof of purpose, proof of causation, and of neat correspondence, as in the *Dayton*[18] case, between identified violation and permissible remedial obligation, with no further remedial obligation. Except in the narrowest and limited sense, there is no concern for results. In effect, the Supreme Court, or the consciousness of antidiscrimination law, seems to be saying, as some of you may recall Phil Ochs tried to say about the Vietnam War, that the "war is over," because we declare that it's over, and for no other reason. To accompany that declaration, some other patterns have emerged, which lead into the question of educational alternatives.

The basic task of the era of rationalization has been to remind everyone that the concept of violation in civil rights law is a very narrow one, strictly in accordance with the perpetrator perspective.[19] Along with that effort, some new ideas have emerged. One I call the "remedial counterpoint." Having narrowed the concept of violation, the Court is willing to tolerate at least, and perhaps to insist upon, intensive remedial efforts, beyond what has previously been expected. The best example is the "educational components" upheld by the Court in *Milliken II*.[20] Since the one thing not available as remedy in that concededly segregated system was desegregation in fact, the Court upheld these special educational remedies in what remains a very perplexing case, since the members of the Court disagreed as to whether the remedies being upheld were to be regarded as mandatory or voluntarily initiated. The question of how mandatory such remedies will be remains to be worked out. The case suggests that it may be possible to seize upon a pose of the law that must keep up the image of the great remedial vigilance in the ever more narrow areas of violation. The implicit message is that pragmatic alternatives may be available while traditional remedial goals remain more distant than ever.

The other notion, which has possibly been eroded by *Bakke* (but probably just made a little more difficult), is voluntarism. The idea is that conditions that will not be deemed violations of law may nevertheless be remediable through voluntary action. If you can convince the school board, then go ahead. The Court has said as much in *Swann*, as part of its insistence on perpetrator form, when it reminded us that the Constitution did not require racial balance but noted that a school board could try to achieve that goal if it wished to as a matter of educational policy. And a number of opinions in *United Jewish Organizations* v. *Carey*,[21] a voting rights case, seem to underscore the voluntarism principle. To relegate the remedy of conditions to the tentative world of voluntarism, of course, reinforces the dissonance between the experience of burden imposed on those whites who are called upon to participate in such programs and the felt innocence of such persons created by the perpetrator perspective. And *Bakke* shows how voluntarism can be manipulated, can be made tantalizingly elusive by increasing its attendant costs.

The major accomplishment of the era of rationalization has been to eradicate the victim perspective from the expectations created by antidiscrimination law. Its most significant case is not *Bakke*, which at most involved the permissible limits of voluntarism, but *Washington* v. *Davis*,[22] which illustrates how conditions associated with discrimination from the victim perspective can be rationalized into future society by presuming their validity rather than demanding their justification. That case, which affects all constitutional antidiscrimination law (and may affect the statutory domain as well), along with the *Pasadena*[23] case for schools, the *Beer*[24] case for voting, and the *Teamsters*[25] case for employment, serves to reaffirm the view that results are ultimately irrelevant.

III. RACE, CLASS, AND EQUALITY OF OPPORTUNITY

If I were content to stay within the structure of legal ideology and argument, I would write a brief in favor of the victim perspective as the appropriate norm for judicial decision-making in racial discrimination cases. But somehow I feel sure that the law's refusal to incorporate the victim perspective had little to do with either the logic of legal argument or the subjective wishes of the participants in the legal process. Suppose one drops the simplistic model, presupposed by much discussion about antidiscrimination law, of "white" society and "black" society, and replaces it with a social structure characterized more by conflict than consensus, by class structure than by community of interest, by relations of domination and exploitation than by relations of cooperation or mutual benefit.

In such a social structure, which I believe corresponds more closely with the real one, the basic contours of the rejection of the victim perspective, including both the fact and the manner of its rejection, can be understood as corresponding with the interests of a ruling class in a class society—can be understood as an instance of law as legitimation of the existing class structure. The doctrinal developments occurred largely through the internal tensions and dynamics of legal thought, without the guiding hand of either history or a conspiratorial elite, and with setbacks, interruptions, and mistakes. In addition, both the forms adopted by law as legitimation and legitimated by the process are complex and contradictory, and cannot be squeezed into linear progressions. With these qualifications as a backdrop, I offer a tentative outline of antidiscrimination law regarded as law as legitimation.

During the period of doctrinal evolution, civil rights law moved from the frankly racist freedom of association view, to the neutral, clean-looking, positivist "color-blind" view, to the modern perpetrator perspective, which has offered minimal (more than none) results while seeming to struggle against the moral force of the color-blind theory. Despite that struggle, however, the modern perpetrator perspective serves to legitimize (legally and morally) the major institutions that maintain a disproportionate number of black people as an underclass.

It is difficult to believe that a large black underclass is still needed as a strictly economic matter. Given technological change, not to mention the available pool of illegal aliens, there would seem no economic obstacle to the disappearance (through assimilation) of American blacks as an identifiably burdened group. Moreover, one might suppose that ever since World War II, as suggested by publications such as Gunnar Myrdal's *An American Dilemma,* it has been the case that nothing would be better for the defender of the "free world" who had conquered Fascist Racism than to obliterate the scars of its own racism. This becomes all the more plausible to the extent the American ruling class incorporated its own antiracist ideology as it evolved.

In these terms, making the problem of race go away would involve no more than the "bourgeoisification" of American blacks in sufficient numbers to take away their identity as an historical victim class. It also seems that, from the perspective of the 1950s, race was (and largely still is) a separate and unique problem of oppression, with its own ideology and structure of relationships complementary to the class structure generally. And the promise of racial liberation never had to implicate the class structure generally, at least in theory. The question then is whether the doctrine as it has evolved—to rationalize rather than liberate—is in fact in the self-interest of the ruling class at all.

An immediate (but only partially satisfactory, if that) answer is to suggest that while racism in the presence of an exploited racial underclass has outlived its usefulness, racism as a necessarily divisive ideology for blocking access to class consciousness remains rationally useful to keep the class structure intact. Without in any way denying the experiential validity of racism as a continuing lived ideology, or even denying the potential benefits in divisiveness to be gained from that fact, I still find the argument lacking in force. Given the benefits in world credibility, not to mention the potential allegiance of a large American black population to be drawn into the legitimation process itself, to posit a *need* for that divisiveness to support the class structure seems to underestimate the pervasive effect of other established ideologies that do the same job (e.g., the "liberal tradition").

It may be that the divisiveness factor better explains retrenchment stemming from a fear of *too much* divisive behavior. This view suggests that the real danger to the ruling class is too much intraclass hostility along racial lines rather than too little, especially to the extent that hostility among lower-class whites breeds the conditions for a genuine threat to stability like demagogic fascism.

So why was the victim perspective rejected? Ambiguous in application though consistent in form, the perpetrator perspective, through manipulation of remedy, offered substantial promises of liberation during the era of contradiction. As I suggested earlier, a combination of impatience, fear of embarrassment, or desire for some results (rather than none) gave rise through resultant ideological forms to an expectation that incorporated the victim perspective. Is one to regard the subsequent rejection of the victim perspective (which, in a sense, had never been accepted formally) as a mere accident resulting from the fortuitous appointment of the Burger court, or as symptomatic of a deeper structural problem? While the timing of individual decisions may be regarded as fortuitous, there seems a deep structural explanation for the jurisprudence of cure—one that forces a convergence of race and class.

In at least three ways, needs basic to preservation of the class structure (not "American society," but the particular class relationships characteristic of contemporary American society) compel rejection of the victim perspective. The first is the problem of formal equality, compounded by the legacy of blatant racism. A remedy that requires change in practical conditions must have some dislocative impact. And a regime of formal equality will insure that the dislocative impact is disproportionately borne by lower-class whites (not to mention blacks, who are burdened either way). The best metaphor and concrete expression of this problem is the issue of the rich senators who favor busing while sending their own kids to fancy private schools. Contemplate a legal response that would *require participation of those children* in a busing plan. Measure the gap between that sort of legal response and that which is contained by the limits of legal ideology (think of the abstract universals to be hauled out in opposition—privacy, freedom of association, family autonomy, and others). To argue that the remedial structure must necessarily overburden the ruling class is to meet the rigor of formal equality, which knows no such concepts, and necessarily burdens lower classes. This problem leads to hostility and instability, which only coercive force can contain. Two other problems threaten essential structures of legitimation.

The second is a basic presupposition of legal ideology and of the existing class structure—the legitimacy of vested rights. The idea that vested rights might be treated as undeserved and therefore taken back

directly (rather than through taxation, which is sufficiently manipul-
able to be nonthreatening) was probably too dangerous to be let out of
confinement for very long. The threat that racial remediation required
sacrifice of vested interests appeared in a variety of contexts—it's
another way of looking at the private school issue, and it's even more
significant in the seniority cases and the sanctity-of-the-suburbs cases.

The perpetrator perspective does not threaten vested rights, since
it presupposes the innocence of those not implicated, and the legitimacy of positions of advantage previously obtained. The victim perspective, by unleashing its force against *conditions* rather than practices,
threatens the legitimacy of vested rights while tarnishing the "innocence" of holders. But the principle of "no retroactivity" or "protection
of expectations" is central to protecting and insulating vested rights,
with exceptions requiring the most extraordinary justification. For
example, the moratorium on mortgage foreclosures was upheld during the 1930s depression in the *Blaisdell* case. There the principle could
be violated to save capitalism. The era of contradiction exerted great
pressure on the ideology of vested rights, though it pretended to be
dealing with perpetrators, as, for example, when the Court in *Swann*
and *Keyes* defeated "expectations" of neighborhood school assignment,
while lower courts invalidated seniority systems.

A full-fledged adoption of the victim perspective destroys the
presupposition of legitimacy of vested rights. All positions of advantage become potentially illegitimate. Formal equality, of course, in-
sures that the positions of advantage belonging to lower classes will be
sacrificed first (and the process will likely go no further), but at risk to
the idea of legitimacy. By reasserting its requirements of causation and
individual responsibility, the perpetrator perspective reestablishes the
presupposition of legitimacy with respect to vested rights.

The third structural feature protected by the perpetrator perspective is the myth of equality of opportunity. Equality of opportunity
presents itself as both a description and a transcendent ideal. It in-
corporates the twin universals of personal desert (self-fulfillment) and
societal advantage (maximize the product). In either form, with its two
universals, it presupposes a world of atomistic individuals, without a
class structure. But most of all it presupposes an objective, transcendent notion of merit or qualification. However much one debunks the
lived reality of this myth (and great supportive forces operate to make
up for its weaknesses—e.g., concepts of luck or fate), I suggest that
duality of opportunity is neither a description nor an ideal but an
ideology with supporting practices—an ideology that is the major
rationalization of class domination in this country. Central to its effectiveness is the lived, internalized experience of class status (lower) as

personal failure, as lack of ability. For this ideology to remain effective, there must be a credible, objective, positivist notion of "qualification."

But how can an ideology that serves to rationalize a system of class commination be expected to function as if it were an ideal? One discovers a gap so wide between the idea of equality of opportunity and its practical realization as to debunk it as a practice, unless the idea of "merit" works to legitimize class relationships. The *Griggs* case was the most radical case of the era of contradiction, insofar as it dropped the presupposition that equality of opportunity was in fact working in the case of tests (which are both a concrete expression of, and the most powerful metaphor of, meritocracy). *Griggs* demanded no more than that equality of opportunity be demonstrated as working in its own terms—that people who could do things best were, in fact, being chosen to do them.

The scrutiny of testing opened up by this radical doctrine leads one to discover that tests are either irrational or meaningless (in that they correlate best with other tests, but rarely with the underlying task for which the prediction is being made, assuming the remote possibility that the underlying task can be satisfactorily "measured" or "quantified"); or to discover that tests can best be regarded as rational if perceived as an intergenerational device for class cloning. To discover the latter is to perceive equality of opportunity as ideology, and to perceive once again a purportedly objective structure as reflecting the narrower interest of dominant classes. All of this becomes reinforced if one pursues the history and origins of testing in the United States, and the continuing politics of "intelligence."[27]

The more that civil rights law threatened the "system" of equality of opportunity, which threat was essential to the production of victim perspective results, the more it threatened to expose and delegitimize the relative situation of lower-class whites. The response of the era of rationalization was to restore, with *Washington* v. *Davis*, the protective insulation of presupposition around testing, to facilitate a return to the basic outlook of equality of opportunity—"blaming the victim." Thus the spirit of the current period is to maintain the appearance of remedial effort while securing the hegemony of crucial presuppositions. In this context, the movement for "effective education," however pragmatic the impulse behind it, operates to place responsibility on "victims" while presupposing a structure of equality of opportunity ready to receive them. Similarly, I perceive academic efforts to denounce the worth of busing, extol segregated schools as representative of "American pluralism," and recast the issue of *Brown* as never having had to do with anything but the measurable "effectiveness" of education, as, however sincerely offered, a structural part of the same process of rationalization represented by the recent Supreme Court cases.

To achieve the kind of massive results demanded by the victim perspective requires suspension of the equality of opportunity ideology for a time sufficient to "bourgeoisify" vast numbers of black people, while maintaining that ideology simultaneously for everyone else, lest the legitimacy of the entire class structure be threatened. To avoid the potential for instability in continuing such a course of action, legal ideology had to reject the victim perspective. The present goal would seem to be to legitimize the accomplishments of civil rights law by emphasizing and displaying a small but successful black middle class, and seeking to gain its allegiance while ignoring the victim perspective claims of the vast and disproportionate numbers of poor and unemployed black people.

Thus, despite the uniqueness of race as an historical problem of oppression, it cannot be remedied alone unless one is willing to accept nothing more than token bourgeoisification within the structure of a presupposed system of equality of opportunity—in short, one must become part of the legitimation process. To challenge that limited view is to tackle the pretense of equality of opportunity directly, and to see it for what it is in relation to class structure.

NOTES

1. Regents of the Univ. of Cal. v. Bakke, 438 U.S. 265 (1978).
2. Brown v. Board of Education, 347 U.S. 483 (1954) (Brown I).
3. See generally W. RYAN, BLAMING THE VICTIM (paperback ed. 1976). See also H. Gutman, *The Black Family in Slavery and Freedom, 1750–1925*, at xvii-xxii (1976).
4. 418 U.S. 717 (1974).
5. Black, *The Lawfulness of the Segregation Decisions*, 69 YALE L.J. 421 (1960); *accord*, Cahn, *Jurisprudence*, 30 N.Y.U. L. REV. 150, 159–60 (1955).
6. Plessy v. Ferguson, 163 U.S. 537, 559 (Harlan, J., dissenting).
7. Regents of the Univ. of Cal. v. Bakke, 438 U.S. 265 (opinion of Powell, J., announcing the judgment of the Court).
8. 380 U.S. 202 (1965).
9. Green v. County School Bd., 391 U.S. 430 (1968).
10. Monroe v. Board of Comm'rs, 391 U.S. 450 (1968).
11. Swann v. Charlotte-Mecklenburg Bd. of Educ., 402 U.S. 1 (1971).
12. Wright v. Council of Emporia, 407 U.S. 451 (1972).
13. Keyes v. School District No. 1, 413 U.S. 189 (1973). For a discussion of the school cases, see Fiss, *School Desegregation: The Uncertain Path of the Law*, 4 PHILOSOPHY & PUB. AFF. 3, 15–35 (1974). I am indebted to the analysis in this discussion.

14. Quoted in R. Kluger, *Simple Justice* 572 (1976).
15. 401 U.S. 424 (1971).
16. See, e. g., International Bhd. of Teamsters v. United States, 431 U.S. 324, 348–55 (1977); General Elec. Co. v. Gilbert, 429 U.S. 125, 137–46 (1976); Washington v. Davis, 426 U.S. 229, 238–39, 248–52 (1976).
17. 418 U.S. 717 (1974).
18. Dayton Bd. of Educ. v. Brinkman, 433 U.S. 406 (1977). See Pasadena City Bd. of Educ. v. Spangler, 427 U.S. 424 (1976).
19. The principal case is Washington v. Davis, 426 U.S. 229 (1976). Its counterpart in legal scholarship is Brest, *The Supreme Court, 1975 Term—Foreword: In Defense of the Antidiscrimination Principle*, 90 HARV. L. REV. 1 (1976).
20. Milliken v. Bradley, 433 U.S. 267 (1977).
21. 430 U.S. 144 (1977).
22. 426 U.S. 229 (1976).
23. Pasadena City Bd. of Educ. v. Spangler, 427 U.S. 424 (1976).
24. Beer v. United States, 425 U.S. 130 (1976).
25. International Bhd. of Teamsters v. United States, 431 U.S. 324 (1977).
26. For an exceptional treatment of this subject, see R. SENNETT and J. COBB, THE HIDDEN INJURIES OF CLASS (1973).
27. See, e.g., S. Gould, *Ever Since Darwin* 243–47 (1977); D. TYACK, THE ONE BEST SYSTEM 204–29 (1974); BOWLES AND GINTIS, *I.Q. in the U.S. Class Structure*, SOC. POL'Y, November–December 1972 and January–February 1973, at 65–96.

CHAPTER SIX

Those scholars who hailed the Supreme Court's *Brown* decision were not impressed by Professor Herbert Wechsler's suggestion that while the decision was welcome, the Court's opinion was deficient in failing to identify a neutral principle of law on which the result could be justified through analysis and reasons that transcended the decision itself.

Spurred to reexamine the Wechsler thesis by the increasing judicial resistance to school desegregation remedies, it is possible to discern a pattern of decisions in race cases that offer remedies for racial discrimination when those remedies tend to secure or advance the interests of the society's upper classes.

If the interest-convergence findings discussed here are accurate and the recognition of black rights depends on the presence of white interests, the conclusions that follow conform quite closely to Alan Freeman's less than optimistic predictions about the future of the struggle against racism in schools and elsewhere. But the very existence of *Brown* suggests that the historic precedent may yet be implemented by the adoption of educationally oriented remedies that avoid or minimize racial-interest conflict while utilizing the still impressive legal and moral force of *Brown* to gain effective schooling for minority children in the schools they now attend.

BROWN AND THE INTEREST-CONVERGENCE DILEMMA

In 1954, the Supreme Court handed down the landmark decision *Brown* v. *Board of Education,*[1] in which the Court ordered the end of state-mandated racial segregation of public schools. Now, more than twenty-five years after that dramatic decision, it is clear that *Brown* will not be forgotten. It has triggered a revolution in civil rights law and in the political leverage available to blacks in and out of court. As Judge Robert L. Carter put it, *Brown* transformed blacks from beggars pleading for decent treatment under the law as their constitutionally recognized right.[2]

Yet today, most black children attend public schools that are both racially isolated and inferior.[3] Demographic patterns, white flight, and the inability of the courts to effect the necessary degree of social reform render further progress in implementing *Brown* almost impossible. The late Professor Alexander Bickel warned that *Brown* would not be overturned but, for a whole array of reasons, "may be headed for— dread word—irrelevance."[4] Bickel's prediction is premature in law where the *Brown* decision remains viable, but it may be an accurate assessment of its current practical value to millions of black children who have not experienced the decision's promise of equal educational opportunity.

Shortly after *Brown,* Professor Herbert Wechsler rendered a sharp and nagging criticism of the decision.[5] Though he welcomed its result, he criticized its lack of a principled basis. Professor Wechsler's views have since been persuasively refuted,[6] yet within them lie ideas that may help to explain the disappointment of *Brown* and what can be done to renew its promise.

In this essay, I plan to take a new look at Wechsler within the context of the subsequent desegregation campaign. By doing so, I hope to offer an explanation of why school desegregation has in large part failed and what can be done to bring about change.

I. PROFESSOR WECHSLER'S SEARCH
FOR NEUTRAL PRINCIPLES IN BROWN

The year was 1959, five years after the Supreme Court's decision in *Brown*. If there was anything the hard-pressed partisans of the case did not need, it was more criticism of a decision ignored by the president, condemned by much of Congress and resisted wherever it was sought to be enforced.[7] Certainly, civil rights adherents did not welcome adding to the growing list of critics the name of Professor Herbert Wechsler, an outstanding lawyer, a frequent advocate for civil rights causes, and a scholar of prestige and influence.[8] Nevertheless, Professor Wechsler chose that time and an invitation to deliver Harvard Law School's Oliver Wendell Holmes Lecture as the occasion to raise new questions about the legal appropriateness of *Brown* and several other major civil rights decisions.[9]

Here was an attack that could not be dismissed as after-the-fact faultfinding by a conservative academician using his intellect to further a preference for keeping blacks in their "separate-but-equal" place. Professor Wechsler began by saying that he had welcomed the result in *Brown;* he noted that he had joined with the NAACP's Charles Houston in litigating civil rights cases in the Supreme Court.[10] He added that he was certainly not upset because the Court overturned earlier decisions approving segregated schools. That the departure from past precedents disturbed settled patterns in a position of the country did not, Wechsler felt, constitute legitimate criticism. Nor was he persuaded by the argument that the issue should have been left to Congress because the Court's judgment might not be honored.[11]

Wechsler did not align himself with the "realists," who "perceive in law only the element of fiat, in whose conception of the legal cosmos reason has no meaning or no place,"[12] nor with the "formalists," who "frankly or covertly make the test of virtue in interpretation whether its result in the immediate decision seems to hinder or advance the interests or the values they support."[13] Wechsler instead saw the need for criteria of decision that could be framed and tested as an exercise of reason and not merely adopted as an act of willfulness or will. He believed, in short, that courts could engage in a "principled appraisal" of legislative actions that exceeded a fixed "historical meaning" of constitutional provisions without, as Judge Learned Hand feared, becoming "a third legislative chamber."[14] Courts, Wechsler argued, "must be genuinely principled," with every step that is involved in reaching judgment resting on "analysis and reasons quite transcending the immediate result that is achieved."[15] Applying these standards, which included constitutional and statutory interpretation, the subtle guidance provided by history, and appropriate but not slavish fidelity to precedent, Wechsler found difficulty with Supreme Court decisions where principled reasoning was in his view either deficient or, in some instances, nonexistent.[16] He included the *Brown* opinion in the latter category.

Wechsler reviewed and rejected the possibility that *Brown* was based on a declaration that the Fourteenth Amendment barred all racial lines in legislation.[17] He also doubted that the opinion relied upon a factual determination that segregation caused injury to black children, since evidence as to such harm was both inadequate and conflicting.[18] Rather, Wechsler concluded, the Court in *Brown* must have rested its holding on the view that "racial segregation is, *in principle*, a denial of equality to the minority against whom it is directed; that is, the group that is not dominant politically and, therefore, does not make the choice involved."[19] Yet, Wechsler found this argument untenable as well, because, among other difficulties, it seemed to require an inquiry into the motives of the legislature, a practice generally foreclosed to the courts.[20]

After dismissing these arguments, Wechsler then asserted that the legal issue in state-imposed segregation cases was not one of discrimination at all, but rather of associational rights: "the denial by the state of freedom to associate, a denial that impinges in the same way on any groups or races that may be involved."[21] Wechsler reasoned that "if the freedom of association is denied by segregation, integration forces an association upon those for whom it is unpleasant or repugnant."[22] And concluding with a question that has challenged legal scholars, Wechsler asked:

> Given a situation where the state must practically choose between denying the association to those individuals who wish it or imposing it on those who would avoid it, is there a basis in neutral principles for holding that the Constitution demands that the claims for association should prevail?[23]

In suggesting that there was a basis in neutral principles for holding that the Constitution supports a claim by blacks for an associational right, Professor Wechsler confessed that he had not yet written an opinion supporting such a holding. "To write it is for me the challenge of the school-segregation cases."[24]

II. THE SEARCH FOR A NEUTRAL PRINCIPLE: RACIAL EQUALITY AND INTEREST CONVERGENCE

Scholars who accepted Professor Wechsler's challenge had little difficulty finding a neutral principle on which the *Brown* decision could be based. Indeed, from the hindsight of a quarter century of the greatest racial consciousness-raising the country has ever known, much of Professor Wechsler's concern seems hard to imagine. To doubt that racial segregation is harmful to blacks, and to suggest that what blacks really sought was the right to associate with whites, is to believe in a world that does not exist now and could not possibly have existed then. Professor Charles Black, therefore, correctly viewed racial equality as the neutral principle that underlay the *Brown* opinion.[25] In Black's view, Wechsler's question "is awkwardly simple,"[26] and he states his response in the form of a syllogism. Black's major premise is that "the equal protection clause of the fourteenth amendment should be read as saying that the Negro race, as such, is not to be significantly disadvantaged by the laws of the states."[27] His minor premise is that "segregation is a massive intentional disadvantaging of the Negro race, as such, by state law."[28] The conclusion, then, is that the equal protection clause clearly bars racial segregation because segregation harms blacks and benefits whites in ways too numerous and obvious to require citation.[29]

Logically, the argument is persuasive, and Black has no trouble urging that "[w]hen the directive of equality cannot be followed without displeasing the white[s], then something that can be called a 'freedom' of the white[s] must be impaired."[30] It is precisely here, though, that many whites part company with Professor Black. Whites may agree in the abstract that blacks are citizens and are entitled to constitutional protection against racial discrimination, but few are willing to recognize that racial segregation is much more than a series of quaint customs that can be remedied effectively without altering the status of whites. The extent of this unwillingness is illustrated by the controversy over affirmative action programs, particularly those where identifiable whites must step aside for blacks they deem less qualified or less deserving. Whites simply cannot envision the personal responsibility and the potential sacrifice inherent in Professor Black's conclusion that true equality for blacks will require the surrender of racism-granted privilege for whites.

This sober assessment of reality raises concern about the ultimate import of Black's theory. On a normative level, as a description of how the world *ought* to be, the notion of racial equality appears to be the proper basis on which *Brown* rests, and Wechsler's framing of the problem in terms of associatonal rights thus seems misplaced. Yet, on a positivistic level—how the world *is*—it is clear that racial equality is not deemed legitimate by large segments of the American people, at least to the extent it threatens to impair the societal status of whites. Hence, Wechsler's search for a guiding principle in the context of associational rights retains merit in the positivistic sphere, because it suggests a deeper truth about the subordination of law to interest-group politics with a racial configuration.

Although no such subordination is apparent in *Brown*, it is possible to discern in more recent school decisions the outline of a principle, applied without direct acknowledgment, that could serve as the positivist expression of the neutral statement of general applicability sought by Professor Wechsler. Its elements rely as much on political history as legal precedent and emphasize the world as it is rather than how we might want it to be. Translated from judicial activity in racial cases both before and after *Brown*, this principle of "interest convergence" provides:

The interest of blacks in achieving racial equality will be accommodated only when it converges with the interests of whites; however, the fourteenth amendment, standing alone, will not authorize a judicial remedy providing effective racial equality for blacks where the remedy sought threatens the superior societal status of middle- and upper-class whites.

It follows that the availability of Fourteenth Amendment protection in racial cases may not actually be determined by the character of harm suffered by blacks or the quantum of liability proved against whites. Racial remedies may instead be the outward manifestations of unspoken and perhaps subconscious judicial conclusions that the remedies, if granted, will secure, advance, or at least not harm societal interests deemed important by middle- and upper class whites. Racial justice—or its appearance—may, from time to time, be counted among the interests deemed important by the courts and by society's policymakers.

In assessing how this principle can accommodate both the *Brown* decision and the subsequent development of school desegregation law, it is necessary to remember that the issue of school segregation and the harm it inflicted on black children did not first come to the Court's attention in the *Brown* litigation: blacks had been attacking the validity of these policies for 100 years.[31] Yet, prior to *Brown*, black claims that segregated public schools were inferior had been met by orders requiring merely that facilities be made equal.[32] What accounted, then, for the sudden shift in 1954 away from the separate but equal doctrine and towards a commitment to desegregation?

I contend that the decision in *Brown* to break with the Court's long-held position on these issues cannot be understood without some consideration of the decision's value to whites, not simply those concerned about the immorality of racial inequality, but also those whites in policymaking positions able to see the economic and political advances at home and abroad that would follow abandonment of segregation.

First, the decision helped to provide immediate credibility to America's struggle with Communist countries to win the hearts and minds of emerging third-world peoples. At least this argument was advanced by lawyers for both the NAACP and the federal government.[33] And the point was not lost on the news media. *Time* magazine, for example, predicted that the international impact of *Brown* would be scarcely less important than its effect on the education of black children: "In many countries, where U.S. prestige and leadership have been damaged by the fact of U.S. segregation, it will come as a timely reassertion of the basic American principle that 'all men are created equal.' "[34]

Second, *Brown* offered much needed reassurance to American blacks that the precepts of equality and freedom so heralded during World War II might yet be given meaning at home. Returning black veterans faced not only continuing discrimination, but also violent attacks in the South that rivalled those that took place at the conclusion of World War I.[35] Their disillusionment and anger were poignantly expressed by the black actor Paul Robeson, who in 1949 declared: "It is unthinkable . . . that American Negroes would go to war on behalf of those who have oppressed us for generations . . . against a country [the Soviet Union] which in one generation has raised our people to the full human dignity of mankind."[36] It is not impossible to imagine that fear of the spread of such sentiment influenced subsequent racial decisions made by the courts.

Finally, there were whites who realized that the South could make the transition from a rural, plantation society to the sunbelt with all its potential and profit only when it ended its struggle to remain divided by state-sponsored segregation.[37] Thus, segregation was viewed as a barrier to further industrialization in the South.

These points may seem insufficient proof of self-interest leverage to produce a decision as important as *Brown*. They are cited, however, to help assess and not to diminish the Supreme Court's most important statement on the principle of racial equality. Here, as in the abolition of slavery, there were whites for whom recognition of the racial equality principle was sufficient motivation. But, as with abolition, the number who would act on morality alone was insufficient to bring about the desired racial reform.[38]

Thus, for those whites who sought an end to desegregation on moral grounds or for the pragmatic reasons outlined above, *Brown* appeared to be a welcome break with the past. When segregation was finally condemned by the Supreme Court, however, the outcry was nevertheless great, especially among poorer whites who feared loss of control over their public schools and other facilities. Their fear of loss was intensified by the sense that they had been betrayed. They relied, as had generations before them, on the expectation that white elites would maintain lower-class whites in a societal status superior to that designated for blacks.[39] In fact, there is evidence that segregated schools and facilities were initially established by legislatures at the insistence of the white working class.[40] Today, little has changed. Many poorer whites oppose social reform as "welfare programs for blacks" although, ironically, they have employment, education, and social service needs that differ from those of poor blacks by a margin that, without a racial scorecard, is difficult to measure.[41]

Unfortunately, poorer whites are now not alone in their opposition to school desegregation and to other attempts to improve the societal status of blacks: recent decisions, most notably by the Supreme Court, indicate that the convergence of black and white interests that led to *Brown* in 1954 and influenced the character of its enforcement has begun to fade. In *Swann* v. *Charlotte-Mecklenburg Board of Education*,[42] Chief Justice Burger spoke of the "reconciliation of competing values" in desegregation cases.[43] If there was any doubt that "competing values" referred to the conflicting interests of blacks seeking desegregation and whites who prefer to retain existing school policies, then the uncertainty was dispelled by *Milliken* v. *Bradley*,[44] and by *Dayton Board of Education* v. *Brinkman (Dayton I)*.[45] In both cases, the Court elevated the concept of "local autonomy" to a "vital national tradition":[46] "No single tradition in public education is more deeply rooted than local control over the operation of schools; local autonomy has long been thought essential both to the maintenance of community concern and support for public schools and to quality of the educational process."[47] Local control, however, may result in the maintenance of a status quo that will preserve superior educational opportunities and facilities for whites at the expense of Blacks. As one commentator has suggested, "It is implausible to assume that school boards guilty of substantial violations in the past will take the interests of black school children to heart."[48]

As a result of its change in attitudes, the Court has increasingly erected barriers to achieving the forms of racial balance relief it earlier had approved.[49] Plaintiffs must now prove that the complained-of segregation was the result of discriminatory actions intentionally and invidiously conducted or authorized by school officials.[50] It is not enough that segregation was the "natural and foreseeable" consequence of their policies.[51] And even when this difficult standard of proof is met, courts must carefully limit the relief granted to the harm actually proved.[52] Judicial second thoughts about racial balance plans with broad-range busing components, the very plans that civil rights lawyers have come to rely on, is clearly evident in these new proof standards.

There is, however, continuing if unpredictable concern in the Supreme Court about school boards whose policies reveal long-term adherence to overt racial discrimination. In many cases, trial courts exposed to exhaustive testimony regarding the failure of school officials to either desegregate or provide substantial equality of schooling for minority children, become convinced that the school boards are violating *Brown*. Thus far, unstable Supreme Court majorities have upheld broad desegregation plans ordered by these judges,[53] but the reservations expressed by concurring justices[54] and the vigor of those justices who dissent[55] caution against optimism in this still controversial area of civil rights law.[56]

At the very least, these decisions reflect a substantial and growing divergence in the interests of whites and blacks. The result could prove to be the realization of Professor Wechsler's legitimate fear that, if there is not a change of course, the purported entitlement of whites not to associate with blacks in public schools may yet eclipse the hope and the promise of *Brown*.

III. INTEREST-CONVERGENCE REMEDIES UNDER BROWN

Further progress to fulfill the mandate of *Brown* is possible to the extent that the divergence of racial interest can be avoided or minimized. Whites in policymaking positions, including those who sit on federal courts, can take no comfort in the conditions of dozens of inner-city school systems where the great majority of nonwhite children attend classes as segregated and ineffective as those so roundly condemned by Chief Justice Warren in the *Brown* opinion. Nor do poorer whites gain from their opposition to the improvement of educational opportunities for blacks: as noted earlier, the needs of the two groups differ little.[57] Hence, over time, all will reap the benefits from a concerted effort toward achieving racial equality.

The question still remains as to the surest way to reach the goal of educational effectiveness for both blacks and whites. I believe that the most widely used programs mandated by the courts—"antidefiance, racial-balance" plans—may in some cases be inferior to plans focusing on "educational components," including the creation and development of "model" all-black schools. A short history of the use of the antidefiance strategy would be helpful at this point.

By the end of the 1950s, it was apparent that compliance with the *Brown* mandate to desegregate the public schools would not come easily or soon. In the seventeen border states and the District of Columbia, fewer than two-hundred thousand blacks were actually attending classes with white children.[58] The states in the deep South had not begun even token desegregation,[59] and it would take Supreme Court action to reverse the years-long effort of the Prince Edward County School Board in Virginia to abolish rather than desegregate its public schools.[60] Supreme Court orders[61] and presidential action had already been required to enable a handful of black students to attend Central High School in Little Rock, Arkansas.[62] Opposition to *Brown* was clearly increasing. Its supporters were clearly on the defensive, as was the Supreme Court itself.

For blacks, the goal in school desegregation suits remained the effective use of the *Brown* mandate to eliminate state-sanctioned segregation. These efforts received unexpected help from the excesses of the massive resistance movement that led courts to justify relief under *Brown* as a reaffirmance of the supremacy of the judiciary on issues of constitutional interpretation. *Brown,* in the view of many, might not have been a wise or proper decision, but violent and prolonged opposition to its implementation posed an even greater danger to the federal system.

The Supreme Court quickly recognized this additional basis on which to ground school desegregation orders. "As this case reaches us," the Court began its dramatic opinion in *Cooper* v. *Aaron,*[63] "it raises questions of the highest importance to the maintenance of our federal system of government."[64] Reaching back to *Marbury* v. *Madison,*[65] the Court reaffirmed Chief Justice Marshall's statement that "It is emphatically the province and duty of the judicial department to say what the law is."[66] There were few opponents to this stand, and Professor Wechsler was emphatically not one of them. His criticism of *Brown* concluded with a denial that he intended to offer "comfort to anyone who claims legitimacy in defiance of the courts."[67] Those who accept the benefits of our constitutional system, Wechsler felt, cannot deny its allegiance when a special burden is imposed. Defiance of court orders, he asserted, constituted the "ultimate negation of all neutral principles."[68]

For some time, then, the danger to federalism posed by the secessionist-oriented resistance of Southern state and local officials provided courts with an independent basis for supporting school desegregation efforts.[69] In the lower federal courts, the perceived threat to judicial status was often quite personal. Surely, I was not the only civil rights attorney who received a favorable decision in a school desegregation case less by legal precedent than because a federal judge— initially hostile to those precedents, my clients, and their lawyer— became incensed with school board litigation tactics that exhibited as little respect for the court as they did for the constitutional rights of black children.

There was a problem with school desegregation decisions framed in this antidefiance form that was less discernible then than now. While a prerequisite to the provision of equal educational opportunity, condemnation of school board evasion was far from synonymous with that long-promised goal. Certainly, it was cause for celebration when the Court recognized that pupil assignment schemes,[70] "freedom-of-choice" plans,[71] and similar "desegregation plans," were in fact designed to retain constitutionally condemned dual-school systems. And, when the Court, in obvious frustration with the slow pace of school desegregation, announced in 1968 what Justice Powell later termed "the *Green/Swann* doctrine of 'affirmative duty,' "[72] which placed on school boards the duty to disestablish their dual-school systems, the decisions were welcomed as substantial victories by civil rights lawyers. Yet, the remedies set forth in the major school cases following *Brown*— balancing the student and teacher populations by race in each school, eliminating one-race schools, redrawing school attendance lines, and transporting students to achieve racial balance[73]—have not in themselves guaranteed black children better schooling than they received in the pre-*Brown* era. Such racial balance measures have often altered the racial appearance of dual school systems without eliminating racial discrimination. Plans relying on racial balance to foreclose evasion have not eliminated the need for further orders protecting black children against discriminatory policies, including resegregation within desegregated schools,[74] the loss of black faculty and administrators,[75] suspensions and expulsions at much higher rates than white students,[76] and varying forms of racial harassment ranging from exclusion from extracurricular activities[77] to physical violence.[78] Antidefiance remedies, then, while effective in forcing alterations in school system structure, often encourage and seldom shield black children from discriminatory retaliation.

The educational benefits that have resulted from the mandatory assignment of black and white children to the same schools are also debatable.[79] If benefits did exist, they have begun to dissipate as whites flee in alarming numbers from school districts ordered to implement mandatory reassignment plans.[80] In response, civil rights lawyers sought to include entire metropolitan areas within mandatory reassignment plans in order to encompass mainly white suburban school districts where so many white parents sought sanctuary for their children.[81]

Thus, the antidefiance strategy was brought full circle from a mechanism for preventing evasion by school officials of *Brown's* antisegregation mandate to one aimed at creating a discrimination-free environment. This approach to the implementation of *Brown*, however, has become increasingly ineffective; indeed, it has in some cases been educationally destructive. A preferable method is to focus on obtaining real educational effectiveness, which may entail the improvement of presently desegregated schools as well as the creation or preservation of model black schools.

Civil rights lawyers do not oppose such relief, but they clearly consider it secondary to the racial balance remedies authorized in the *Swann*[82] and *Keyes*[83] cases. Those who espouse alternative remedies are deemed to act out of suspect motives. *Brown* is the law, and racial balance plans are the only means of complying with *Brown*. The position reflects courage, but it ignores the frequent and often complete failure of programs that concentrate solely on achieving a racial balance.

Desegregation remedies that do not integrate may seem a step backward toward the *Plessy* "separate but equal" era. Some black educators, however, see major educational benefits in schools where black children, parents, and teachers can utilize the real cultural strengths of the black community to overcome the many barriers to educational achievement.[84] As Professor Laurence Tribe argued, "Judicial rejection of the 'separate but equal' talisman seems to have been accompanied by a potentially troublesome lack of sympathy for racial separateness as a possible expression of group solidarity."[85]

This is not to suggest that educationally oriented remedies can be developed and adopted without resistance. Policies necessary to obtain effective schools threaten the self-interest of teacher unions and others with vested interests in the status quo. But successful magnet schools located in black communities may provide a lesson that effective schools for blacks must be a primary goal rather than a secondary result of integration. Many white parents recognize a value in integrated schooling for their children but they quite properly view integration as merely one component of an effective education. To the extent that civil rights advocates also accept this reasonable sense of priority, some greater racial interest conformity should be possible.

*   *   *

Is this what the *Brown* opinion meant by "equal educational opportunity"? Chief Justice Warren said the Court could not "turn the clock back to 1868 when the [fourteenth] Amendment was adopted, or even to 1896 when *Plessy* v. *Ferguson* was written."[86] The change in racial circumstances since 1954 rivals or surpasses all that occurred during the period that preceded it. If the decision that was at least a catalyst for that change is to remain viable, those who rely on it must exhibit the dynamic awareness of all the legal and political considerations that influenced those who wrote it.

Professor Wechsler warned us early on that there was more to *Brown* than met the eye. At one point, he observed that the "opinion is often read with less fidelity by those who praise it than by those whom it is condemned."[87] Most of us openly ignored that observation and quietly raised a question about the sincerity of the observer. Criticism, as we in the movement for minority rights have every reason to learn, is a synonym for neither cowardice nor capitulation. It may instead bring awareness, always the first step toward overcoming still another barrier in the struggle for racial equality.

NOTES

1. 347 U.S. 483 (1954).
2. Carter, *The Warren Court and Desegregation*, in D. BELL, RACE, RACISM AND AMERICAN LAW 456–61 (1973).
3. *See* Bell, Book Review, 92 HARV. L. REV. 1826, 1826 n. 6 (1979). *See also* C. JENCKS, INEQUALITY 27–28 (1972).
4. A. BICKEL, THE SUPREME COURT AND THE IDEA OF PROGRESS 151 (1970).
5. Wechsler, *Toward Neutral Principles of Constitutional Law*, 73 HARV. L. REV. 1 (1959). The lecture was later published in a collection of selected essays. H. WECHSLER, PRINCIPLES, POLITICS, AND FUNDAMENTAL LAW 3 (1961).
6. *See*, e.g., Black, *The Lawfulness of the Segregation Decisions*, 69 YALE L.J. 421 (1960); Heyman, *The Chief Justice, Racial Segregation, and the Friendly Critics*, 49 CALIF. L. REV. 104 (1961); Pollak, *Racial Discrimination and Judicial Integrity: A Reply to Professor Wechsler*, 108 U. PA. L. REV. 1 (1959).
7. The legal campaign that culminated in the *Brown* decision is discussed in

great depth in R. KLUGER, SIMPLE JUSTICE (1976). The subsequent fifteen years is reviewed in S. WASBY, A. D'AMATO, & R. METRAILER, DESEGREGA-TION FROM BROWN TO ALEXANDER (1977).

8. Professor Wechsler is the Harlan Fiske Stone Professor of Constitutional Law Emeritus at the Columbia University Law School. His work is reviewed in 78 COLUM. L. REV. 969 (1978), an issue dedicated in his honor upon his retirement.

9. *See* Wechsler, *supra* note 5, at 31–35.

10. Wechsler recalled that Houston, who was black, "did not suffer more than I in knowing that we had to go to Union Station to lunch together during the recess." *Id.* at 34.

11. *Id.* at 31–32.

12. *Id.* at 11.

13. *Id.*

14. *Id.* at 16.

15. *Id.* at 15.

16. *Id.* at 19.

17. *Id.* at 32.

18. *Id.* at 32–33.

19. *Id.* at 33 (emphasis added).

20. *Id.* at 33–34.

21. *Id.* at 34.

22. *Id.*

23. *Id.*

24. *Id.*

25. *See* Black, *supra* note 6, at 428–29.

26. *Id.* at 421.

27. *Id.*

28. *Id.*

29. *Id.* at 425–26.

30. *Id.* at 429.

31. *See, e.g.,* Roberts v. City of Boston, 59 Mass. (5 Cush.) 198 (1850).

32. The cases are collected in Larson, *The New Law of Race Relations,* 1969 WIS. L. REV. 470, 482–83 n. 27; Leflar & Davis, *Segregation in the Public Schools— 1953,* 67 HARV. L. REV. 377, 430–35 (1954).

33. *See* Bell, *Racial Remediation: An Historical Perspective on Current Conditions,* 52 NOTRE DAME LAW. 5, 12 (1976).

34. *Id.* at 12 n. 31.

35. C. VANN WOODWARD, THE STRANGE CAREER OF JIM CROW 141(3d rev. ed. 1974), J. FRANKLIN, FROM SLAVERY TO FREEDOM 478–86 (3d ed. 1967).

36. D. BUTLER, PAUL ROBESON 137 (1976) (unwritten speech before the Partisans of Peace's World Peace Congress in Paris).

37. Professor Robert Higgs argued that the "region's economic development increasingly undermined the foundations of its traditional racial relations." Higgs, *Race and Economy in the South, 1890–1950,* in THE AGE OF SEGREGATION 89–90 (R. Haws ed. 1978). Sociologists Frances Piven and Richard Cloward have also drawn a connection between this economic

growth and the support for the civil rights movement in the 1940s and 1950s, when various white elites in business, philanthropy, and government began to speak out against racial discrimination. F. PIVEN & R. CLOWARD, REGULATING THE POOR 229–30 (1971). *See also* F. PIVEN AND R. CLOWARD, POOR PEOPLE'S MOVEMENTS 189–94 (1977).

38. President Lincoln, for example, acknowledged the moral evil in slavery. In his famous letter to publisher Horace Greeley, however, he promised to free all, some, or none of the slaves, depending on which policy would most help save the Union. SPEECHES AND LETTERS OF ABRAHAM LINCOLN, 1832–65, at 194–95 (M. Roe ed. 1907).

39. *See* F. PIVEN & R. CLOWARD, POOR PEOPLE'S MOVEMENTS 187 (1977). *See generally* Bell, *supra* note 33.

40. *See* C. VANN WOODWARD, *supra* note 35, at 6.

41. Robert Heilbroner suggests that this country's failure to address social issues including poverty, public health, housing, and prison reform as effectively as many European countries is due to the tendency of whites to view reform efforts as "programs to 'subsidize' Negroes. . . . In such cases the fear and resentment of the Negro takes precedence over the social problem itself. The result, unfortunately, is that the entire society suffers from the results of a failure to correct social evils whose ill effects refuse to obey the rules of segregation." Heilbroner, *The Roots of Social Neglect in the United States,* in IS LAW DEAD? 288, 296 (E. Rostow ed. 1971).

42. 402 U.S. 1 (1971).

43. *Id.* at 31.

44. 418 U.S. 717 (1974) (limits power of federal courts to treat a primarily black urban school district and largely white suburban districts as a single unit in mandating desegregation).

45. 433 U.S. 406 (1977) (desegregation orders affecting pupil assignments should seek only the racial mix that would have existed absent the constitutional violation).

46. 433 U.S. at 410; 418 U.S. at 741–42.

47. 418 U.S. at 741.

48. *The Supreme Court, 1978 Term,* 93 HARV. L. REV. 60, 130, (1979).

49. *See generally* Fiss, *School Desegregation: The Uncertain Path of the Law,* 4 PHILOSOPHY & PUB. AFF. 3 (1974); Kanner, *From Denver to Dayton: The Development of a Theory of Equal Protection Remedies,* 72 NW. U.L. REV. 382 (1977).

50. Dayton Bd. of Educ. v. Brinkman (Dayton I), 433 U.S. 406 (1977).

51. Columbus Bd. of Educ. v. Penick, 99 S. Ct. 2941, 2950 (1979).

52. Austin Independent School Dist. v. United States, 429 U.S. 990, 991 (1976) (Powell, J., concurring).

53. Dayton Bd. of Educ. v. Brinkman (Dayton II), 443 U.S. 526 (1979); Columbus Bd. of Educ. v. Penick, 443 U.S. 449 (1979).

54. *See* Columbus Bd. of Educ. v. Penick, 443 U.S. at 468 (1979) (Burger, C. J., concurring); *id.* at 469 (Stewart, J., concurring).

55. *See id.* at 489 (Rehnquist, J., dissenting); *id.* at 479 (Powell, J., dissenting).

See also Dayton Bd. of Educ. v. Brinkman (Dayton II), 443 U.S. 526, 542 (1979) (Stewart, J., dissenting).

56. The Court evaded another difficult challenge in the 1979 term when it decided not to decide whether the racial balance plan in Dallas, Texas, goes far enough in eliminating one-race schools in a large district that is now 65% black and Hispanic. Tasby v. Estes, 572 F.2d 1010 (5th Cir. 1978), *cert. dismissed as improvidently granted*, Estes v. Metropolitan Branches of Dallas NAACP, 100 S. Ct. 716 (1980). In a dissent joined by Justices Stewart and Rehnquist, Justice Powell indicated he would have decided the case by refusing the further relief sought by the NAACP.

57. *See* TAN 41 *supra.*

58. P. BERGMAN, THE CHRONOLOGICAL HISTORY OF THE NEGRO IN AMERICA 561 (1969).

59. *Id.* at 561–62.

60. Griffin v. County School Bd., 377 U.S. 21–8 (1964).

61. Cooper v. Aaron, 358 U.S. 1 (1958).

62. P. BERGMAN, *supra* note 58, at 555–56, 561–62.

63. 358 U.S. 1 (1958).

64. *Id.* at 4.

65. 5 U.S. (1 Cranch) 137, 177 (1803).

66. 358 U.S. at 18.

67. Wechsler, *supra* note 5, at 35.

68. *Id.*

69. *See,* e.g., Bush v. New Orleans Parish School Bd., 188 F. Supp. 916 (E.D. La.), *aff'd,* 365 U.S. 569 (1961) (invalidation of state "interposition acts"); Poindexter v. Louisiana Financial Comm'n, 275 F. Supp. 833 (E.D. La. 1967), *aff'd per curiam,* 389 U.S. 215 (1968) ("tuition grants" for children attending private, segregated schools voided); Goss v. Board of Educ., 373 U.S. 683 (1963) (struck down "minority to majority" transfer plans enabling resegregation of schools).

70. These plans, requiring black children to run a gauntlet of administrative proceedings to obtain assignment to a white school, were at first judicially approved. Covington v. Edwards, 264 F.2d 780 (4th Cir.), *cert. denied,* 361 U.S. 840 (1959); Shuttlesworth v. Birmingham Bd. of Educ., 162 F.Supp. 372 (N.D. Ala.), *aff'd,* 358 U.S. 101 (1958).

71. Green v. County School Bd., 391 U.S. 430 (1968) (practice of "free choice"—enabling each student to choose whether to attend a black or white school—struck down).

72. Keyes v. School Dist. No. 1, 413 U.S. 189, 224 (1973) (Powell, J., concurring in part and dissenting in part).

73. *See,* e.g., Swann v. Charlotte-Mecklenburg Bd. of Educ., 402 U.S. 1 (1971); Green v. County School Bd., 391 U.S. 430 (1968).

74. *See,* e.g., Jackson v. Marvell School Dist. No. 22, 425 F.2d 211 (8th Cir. 1970). There were also efforts to segregate students within desegregated schools by the use of standardized tests and achievement scores. *See* Singleton v. Jackson Mun. Separate School Dist., 419 F.2d 1211 (5th Cir.), *rev'd*

per curiam, 396 U.S. 290 (1970); Hobson v. Hansen, 269 F.Supp. 401 (D.D.C. 1967), *aff'd sub nom.* Smuck v. Hobson, 408 F.2d 175 (D.C. Cir. 1969).

75. *See,* e.g., Chambers v. Hendersonville City Bd. of Educ., 364 F.2d 189 (4th Cir. 1966). For a discussion of the wholesale dismissal and demotion of black teachers in the wake of school desegregation orders, see materials compiled in 2 N. DORSEN, P. BENDER, B. NEUBORNE, & S. LAW, EMERSON, HABER, AND DORSEN'S POLITICAL AND CIVIL RIGHTS IN THE UNITED STATES 679–80 (4th ed. 1979).

76. Hawkins v. Coleman, 376 F. Supp. 1330 (N.D. Tex. 1974); Dunn v. Tyler Independent School Dist., 327 F. Supp. 528 (E.D. Tex. 1971), *aff'd in part and rev'd in part,* 460 F.2d 137 (5th Cir. 1972).

77. Floyd v. Trice, 490 F.2d 1154 (8th Cir. 1974); Augustus v. School Bd., 361 F. Supp. 383 (N.D. Fla. 1973), *modified,* 507 F.2d 152 (5th Cir. 1975).

78. For an example, see the account of racial violence resulting from desegregation in Boston in Husock, *Boston: The Problem that Won't Go Away,* N.Y. TIMES MAGAZINE 32 (Nov. 25, 1979). *See also* T. COTTLE, BUSING (1976).

79. *See* N. ST. JOHN, SCHOOL DESEGREGATION 16–41 (1975).

80. *See* D. Armor, White Flight, Demographic Transition, and the Future of School Desegregation (1978) (Rand Paper Series, The Rand Corp.); J. Coleman, S. Kelly & J. Moore, Trends in School Segregation, 1968–73 (1975) (Urban Institute Paper). *But see* R. Farley, School Integration and White Flight (1975) (Population Studies Center, U. Mich.); Pettigrew & Green, *School Desegregation in Large Cities: A Critique of the Coleman "White Flight" Thesis,* 46 HARV. EDUC. REV. 1 (1976); Rossell, *School Desegregation and White Flight,* 90 POL. SCI. Q. 675 (1975).

81. *See,* e.g., Milliken v. Bradley, 418 U.S. 717 (1974).

82. Swann v. Charlotte-Mecklenburg Bd. of Educ., 402 U.S. 1 (1971).

83. Keys v. School Dist. No. 1, 413 U.S. 189 (1973).

84. S. LIGHTFOOT, WORLDS APART 172 (1978). For a discussion of the Lightfoot theory, see Bell, *supra* note 3, at 1838.

85. L. TRIBE, AMERICAN CONSTITUTIONAL LAW 16–15, at 1022 (1978) (footnote omitted).

86. 347 U.S. at 492.

87. Wechsler, *supra* note 5, at 32.

Part **IV**

EDUCATIONAL REMEDIES IN PERSPECTIVE

Ronald R. Edmonds
Effective Schools for Minority Children

Derrick Bell
A Model of Alternative Visions

CHAPTER SEVEN

Court-ordered desegregation is, Ron Edmonds believes, a major weapon in the struggle for racial equality, but to the extent that the *Brown* decision is read to deny the potential effectiveness of all-minority schools, much of the decision's force is expended creating and maintaining racially balanced school settings that may be helpful but can prove irrelevant or even detrimental to the educational needs of minority children.

Focusing on schools where low-income minority children are achieving at or above national norms, Mr. Edmonds, Senior Assistant to the Chancellor for Instruction, New York City Public Schools, and a lecturer and research associate at the Harvard Graduate School of Education, identifies characteristics which contribute to impressive student performance, including strong leadership, a positive teaching climate, parental involvement, and emphasis on attaining basic skills. These findings refute the general belief, reinforced by major educational studies, that family background and home environment are the principal causes of quality pupil performance. Social scientists, teachers and courts should not rely on this belief to avoid organizing schools that function effectively for minority children.

It is appropriate to end these essays as they began—with the views of an educator.

EFFECTIVE EDUCATION
FOR MINORITY PUPILS
Brown Confounded or Confirmed

For the last two decades, the *Brown* decision has been the greatest weapon in the black arsenal of civil power. Consider that there are few American cities of any size that have not been profoundly altered as a consequence of black-initiated court-ordered desegregation at the local school district.[1] The history of these class action suits is that they occur as a tactical last resort by a black community that has tried for many years by various means to improve teaching and learning for black children.[2] In fact, school desegregation can best be understood when evaluated in a broader sense as an instrument of instructional reform.[3]

The literature on desegregation is not, for the most part, organized this way, but to be most useful to educational decision-makers should be used this way. Taken as a whole, the research literature says that in and of itself desegregation, defined as the assigning of black and white children to the same schools, has little effect on pupil performance.[4] Even so, the *Brown* mandate offers a unique opportunity to affect educational changes that could not otherwise occur. What must be carefully thought through are those educational changes that will yield the greatest instructional gain for that portion of the pupil population in which we have the greatest interest: those who profit least from existing arrangements. The appropriate reforms will vary from district to district. Thus, in advocating a remedy for racially segregated schools, we will be well prepared to seize the occasion on behalf of a set of reforms that represent the most auspicious use of the circumstances. There may yet be some instances, particularly in small districts, where the percentage of poor minority children is also small, where the best reform may be the actual integration of the schools, achieved by using techniques of racial balance, educational parks, a

Princeton plan, or some other variation intended to effect educational gain through integration.

Racial balance has been the sole remedy of choice for most civil rights lawyers and their supporting organizations, who have not been deterred by the just-cited studies showing that desegregation alone has little effect on pupil performance. There are several reasons for the disappointing achievement figures.

First, our present failure to offer adequate basic education to children of color is confounded by issues of class. Analysis of achievement that focuses on race to the exclusion of class misses the true import of the educational tragedy that presently characterizes public schooling for most black children.

Second, no amount of desegregation will deliver us from our present educational malaise till we change the prevailing public perspective on the interaction between pupil performance and pupil race and family background. We cannot do that unless we confront the profound error that is inherent in most educational research on the origin of achievement.

Third, we must gain an understanding of how poor children of color are even now being properly educated in a number of public schools, and then ask the question: If this is so anywhere, then why not make it so everywhere?

As these three points illustrate, specific issues of demographic desegregation deserve a lower priority when the subject is effective teaching and learning for the children of the poor. In fact, it is my firm belief that, except perhaps in the very small districts previously mentioned, desegregation has exhausted its usefulness as an explicit instrument of instructional reform for black children.

But civil rights advocates adhere to racial balance remedies in substantial part because they have accepted social science data indicating that poor black children are so disadvantaged by their backgrounds that effective schooling is difficult to impossible. In recent years, the most widely disseminated and influential studies of school effects have been James Coleman et al.'s *Equality of Educational Opportunity*[5] and Christopher Jencks et al.'s *Inequality: A Reassessment of the Effect of Family and Schooling in America.*[6] Both books conclude, in sum, that pupil performance is principally caused by family background with the attendant implication that little can be done to increase achievement for poor children. Both studies are profoundly in error in their discussion of the interaction between pupil performance and family background. Most importantly, for their purposes, Coleman and Jencks are mistaken in their conclusion that family background causes pupil performance. School response to family background is in fact the principal determinant of pupil performance.

My subsequent discussion of certain of the literature on school effects must not be taken to mean that whether or not schools are effective derives from matters of research or social science. Such is not the case. Schools teach those they think they must, and when they think they needn't, they don't. That fact has nothing to do with social science except that the children of social scientists are among those that schools feel compelled to teach effectively. There has never been a time in the life of the American public when we have not known all that we needed to teach all those that we chose to teach.

Happily, there is plenty of proof in well-documented, albeit less well-publicized, studies indicating that public schools can effectively educate the children of the poor, including the children of the black poor. These school studies are most explicit in identifying the components of effective education: school organization, instructional strategy, and school community dynamic, all of which seem directly relevant to achievement gains for poor children. Many other school characteristics considered crucial to pupil performance are in fact not important. Indeed, there is ample evidence to justify ignoring a number of school characteristics when our object is instructional reform. First, unless extreme change (less than 15 pupils, more than 35) is being considered, class size, in and of itself, is not a critical variable in determining pupil performance.[7] Class size must of course be considered in any overall instructional strategy but the point is that no appreciable gain in pupil acquisition of basic school skills can be got solely on the basis of a reduction in class size. Let me make clear that for most instructional purposes I prefer small classes to large classes. I recommend small classes for reasons of classroom amiability, ease of management, improved teacher morale and a variety of other important educational interests. Small class size cannot, however, be recommended on the basis of a research literature that predicts greater pupil achievement as a consequence of reduced class size. Similar remarks can be made about school size, teacher experience, teacher's race, teacher's salaries, per pupil expenditure and school facilities.[8] All of these school characteristics are important in a variety of ways for a variety of reasons, but no one of them can be successfully manipulated when the object is greater pupil acquisition of basic school skills.

Let us now examine studies of pupil achievement in urban schools. Weber was an early contributor to the literature on the school determinants of achievement in his 1971 study of four instructionally effective inner-city schools.[9] Weber intended his study to be explicitly alternative to Coleman, Jensen,[10] and other researchers who had satisfied themselves that low achievement by poor children derived principally from inherent disabilities that characterized the poor. Weber focused on the characteristics of four inner-city schools in which reading achievement was clearly successful for poor children on the basis of national norms. All four schools have "strong leadership," in that their principal is instrumental in: setting the tone of the school, helping decide on instructional strategies, and organizing and distributing the school's resources. All four schools have "high expectations" for all their students. Weber is careful to point out that high expectations are not sufficient for school success but they are certainly necessary. All four schools have an orderly, relatively quiet, and pleasant atmosphere. All four schools strongly emphasize pupil acquisition of reading skills and reinforce that emphasis by careful and frequent evaluation of pupil progress.

In 1974, the New York State Office of Education Performance Review published a study[11] that confirmed certain of Weber's major findings. New York identified two inner-city New York City public schools, both of which were serving an analogous, predominantly poor pupil population. One of the schools was high-achieving and the other was low-achieving. Both schools were studied in an attempt to identify those differences that seemed most responsible for the achievement variation between the two schools. The study showed that the differences in student performance in the two schools could be attributed to factors under the schools' control, and that administrative behavior, policies, and practices in the schools appeared to have a significant impact on school effectiveness. In this regard, it was found that the more effective inner-city school was led by an administrative team that provided a good balance between management and instructional skills. In addition, the administrative team in the more effective school had developed a plan for dealing with the reading problem and had implemented the plan throughout the school.

Classroom teachers in both schools had problems in teaching reading and assessing pupils' reading skills, but professional personnel in the less effective school tended to attribute children's reading problems to nonschool factors and were pessimistic about their ability to have an impact; they created an environment in which children failed because they were not expected to succeed. Children responded to unstimulating learning experiences predictably—they were apathetic, disruptive, or absent. In the more effective school, teachers were less skeptical about their ability to have an impact on children.

The authors admitted this study did not identify all factors relating to student reading achievement. They felt, however, that their preliminary findings were consistent with a significant body of other research. While encouraging more research, the authors felt the study had shown that school practices have an effect on reading achievement. "At the very least," they concluded, "the children in low-achieving schools should have the opportunities available to the children of the high-achieving schools. These opportunities, which do not result from higher overall expenditures, are clearly within the reach of any school today."[12]

For our purposes these findings reinforce the relevance of leadership, expectations, and atmosphere as essential institutional elements affecting pupil performance. If further evidentiary support for these findings is wanted, you are invited to close scrutiny of the 1976 Madden, Lawson, Sweet study of school effectiveness in California.[13] In a more rigorous and sophisticated version of the Weber and New York studies, Madden and his colleagues studied 21 pairs of California elementary schools matched on the basis of pupil characteristics and differing only on the basis of pupil performance on standardized achievement measures. The 21 pairs of schools were studied in an effort to identify those institutional characteristics that seemed most responsible for the achievement differences that described the 21 high-achieving schools and the 21 low-achieving schools. The major findings indicated that when compared to teachers at lower-achieving schools, teachers at higher-achieving schools report that their principals provide them with a significantly greater amount of support. Teachers in higher-achieving schools were more task-oriented in their classroom approach and exhibited more evidence of applying appropriate principles of learning than did teachers in lower-achieving schools. The classrooms in higher-achieving schools provided more evidence of student monitoring processes, student effort, happier children, and atmosphere conducive to learning.

In curriculum, the study found teachers at higher-achieving schools spent relatively more time on social studies, less time on mathematics and physical education/health, and about the same amount of time on reading/language development and science as teachers in lower-achieving schools, who tended to use fewer adult volunteers in mathematics classes, more paid aides in reading, and make less use of teacher aides for nonteaching tasks, such as classroom paperwork, watching children on the playground, and maintaining classroom discipline, than teachers in higher-achieving schools. In comparison with grouping practices at lower-achieving schools, the higher-achieving schools divided classrooms into fewer groups for purposes of instruction.

In comparison with teachers at lower-achieving schools, teachers at higher-achieving schools reported higher levels of access to "outside the classroom" materials, and rated district administration higher on support services. These teachers believed their faculty as a whole had less influence on educational decisions. Even so, in comparison with teachers in lower-achieving schools, teachers in higher-achieving schools reported being more satisfied with various aspects of their work.[14]

The California study is chiefly notable for its reinforcement of leadership, expectations, atmosphere, and instructional emphasis as consistently essential institutional determinants of pupil performance.

I want to close this part of the discussion with summary remarks about a recent and unusually persuasive study of school effects. In 1977 W. B. Brookover and L. W. Lezotte published their study of "Changes In School Characteristics Coincident With Changes In Student Achievement."[15] We should take special note of this work partly because it is a formal extension of inquiries and analyses begun in two earlier studies, both of which reinforce certain of the Weber, Madden, et al., and New York findings. The Michigan Department of Education *Cost Effectiveness Study*[16] and the Brookover et al. study of "Elementary School Climate and School Achievement"[17] are both focused on those educational variables that are liable to school control and important to the quality of pupil performance. In response to both of these studies the Michigan Department of Education asked Brookover and Lezotte to study a set of Michigan schools characterized by consistent pupil performance improvement or decline. The Brookover, Lezotte study is broader in scope than the two earlier studies and explicitly intended to profit from methodological and analytical lessons learned in the "Cost Effectiveness . . ." and "Elementary School Climate . . ." studies.

Since the early seventies, the Michigan Department of Education has annually tested all Michigan pupils in public schools in grades four and seven. The tests are criterion-referenced standardized measures of pupil performance in basic school skills. Over time these data were used by the Michigan Department of Education to identify elementary schools characterized by consistent pupil performance improvement or decline. Brookover and Lezotte chose eight of those schools to be studied (six improving, two declining). The schools were visited by trained interviewers who conducted interviews and administered questionnaires to a great many of the school personnel. The interviews and questionnaires were designed to identify differences between the improving and declining schools, which differences seemed most important to the pupil performance variation between the two sets of schools. The following summary gives the results reported by Brookover and

Lezotte in "Changes in School Characteristics Coincident with Changes in Student Achievement":

1. The improving schools are clearly different from the declining schools in the emphasis their staff places on the accomplishment of the basic reading and mathematics objectives. The improving schools accept and emphasize the importance of these goals and objectives while declining schools give much less emphasis to such goals and do not specify them as fundamental.

2. There is a clear contrast in the evaluations that teachers and principals make of the students in the improving and declining schools. The staffs of the improving schools tend to believe that *all* of their students can master the basic objectives; and furthermore, the teachers perceive that the principal shares this belief. They tend to report higher and increasing levels of student ability, while the declining school teachers project the belief that students' ability levels are low and, therefore, they cannot master even these objectives.

3. The staff of the improving schools hold decidedly higher and apparently increasing levels of expectations with regard to the educational accomplishments of their students. In contrast, staff of the declining schools are much less likely to believe that their students will complete high school or college.

4. In contrast to the declining schools, the teachers and principals of the improving schools are much more likely to assume responsibility for teaching the basic reading and math skills and are much more committed to doing so. The staffs of the declining schools feel there is not much that teachers can do to influence the achievement of their students. They tend to displace the responsibility for skill learning on the parents or the students themselves.

5. Since the teachers in the declining schools believe that there is little they can do to influence basic skill learning, it follows they spend less time in direct reading instruction than do teachers in the improving schools. With the greater emphasis on reading and math objectives in the improving schools, the staffs in these schools devote a much greater amount of time toward achieving reading and math objectives.

6. There seems to be a clear difference in the principal's role in the improving and declining schools. In the improving schools, the principal is more likely to be an instructional leader, be more

assertive in his instructional leadership role, is more of a disciplinarian and, perhaps most of all, assumes responsibility for the evaluation of the achievement of basic objectives. The principals in the declining schools appear to be permissive and to emphasize informal and collegial relationships with the teachers. They put more emphasis on general public relations and less emphasis upon evaluation of the school's effectiveness in providing a basic education for the students.

7. The improving school staffs appear to evidence a greater degree of acceptance of the concept of accountability and are further along in the development of an accountability model. Certainly they accept the MEAP tests as one indication of their effectiveness to a much greater degree than the declining-school staffs. The latter tend to reject the relevance of the MEAP tests and make little use of these assessment devices as a reflection of their instruction. (MEAP refers to Michigan Educational Assessment Program.)

8. Generally, teachers in the improving schools are less satisfied than the staffs in the declining schools. The higher levels of reported staff satisfaction and morale in the declining schools seem to reflect a pattern of complacency and satisfaction with the current levels of educational attainment. On the other hand, the improving-school staffs appear more likely to experience some tension and dissatisfaction with the existing condition.

9. Differences in the level of parent involvement in the improving and declining schools are not clear-cut. It seems that there is less overall parent involvement in the improving schools; however, the improving school staffs indicated that their schools have higher levels of *parent-initiated* involvement. This suggests that we need to look more closely at the nature of the involvement exercised by parents. Perhaps parent-initiated contact with the schools represents an effective instrument of educational change.

10. The compensatory education program data suggest differences between improving and declining schools, but these differences may be distorted by the fact that one of the declining schools had just initiated a compensatory education program. In general, the improving schools are not characterized by a high emphasis upon paraprofessional staff, nor heavy involvement of the regular teachers in the selection of students to be placed in compensatory education programs. The declining schools seem to have a great-

er number of different staff involved in reading instruction and more teacher involvement in identifying students who are to be placed in compensatory education programs. The regular classroom teachers in the declining schools report spending more time planning for noncompensatory education reading activities. The decliners also report greater emphasis on programmed instruction.[18]

Before making summary remarks about the policy import of these several studies, I want to say something of my own research, "Search for Effective Schools: The Identification and Analysis of City Schools That Are Instructionally Effective for Poor Children."[19] This discussion will describe our ongoing efforts to identify and analyze city schools that are instructionally effective for poor and/or minority children. I am pleased to note that we have already developed unusually persuasive evidence of the thesis we seek to demonstrate in the research under discussion. Our thesis is that all children are eminently educable, and the behavior of the school is critical in determining the quality of that education.

The "Search for Effective Schools" project began by answering the question: "Are there schools that are instructionally effective for poor children?" In September of 1974, Lezotte, Edmonds, and Ratner described their analysis of pupil performance in the twenty elementary schools that make up Detroit's Model Cities Neighborhood.[20] All of the schools are located in inner-city Detroit and serve a predominantly poor and minority pupil population. Reading and math scores were analyzed from Detroit's Spring 1973 use of the Stanford Achievement Test and the Iowa Test of Basic Skills. Of the 10,000 pupils in the twenty schools in the Model Cities' Neighborhood, 2500 were randomly sampled. With minor variation, the sample included eight pupils per classroom in each of the twenty schools. The mean math and reading scores for the twenty schools were compared with citywide norms. An effective school among the twenty was defined as being at or above the city average grade equivalent in math and reading. An ineffective school was defined as below the city average. Using these criteria, eight of the twenty schools were judged effective in teaching math. Nine were judged effective in teaching reading, and five were judged effective in teaching both math and reading.

We turned next to the problem of establishing the relationship between pupil family background and building effectiveness. Two schools among the twenty, Duffield and Bunche, were found that were matched on the basis of eleven social indicators. Duffield pupils averaged nearly four months above the city average in reading and math.

Bunche pupils averaged nearly three months below the city reading average and 1.5 months below the city math average.

The similarity in the characteristics of the two pupil populations permits us to infer the importance of school behavior in making pupil performance independent of family background. The overriding point here is that, in and of itself, pupil family background neither causes nor precludes elementary school instructional effectiveness.

Despite the value of our early work in Detroit, we recognized the limitations of the Model Cities' Neighborhood analysis. Our evaluation of school success with poor children had depended on evaluating schools with relatively homogeneous pupil populations. The numbers of schools were too few to justify firm conclusions. Finally, the achievement tests were normative, as was the basis for determining building effectiveness among the twenty schools. Even so, valuable lessons were learned in Detroit from which we would later greatly profit.

The second phase of the project was a reanalysis of the 1966 Equal Educational Opportunity Survey (EEOS) data.[21] Our purpose was to answer a number of research questions that required a data base both larger and richer than had been available to us in the Model Cities' Neighborhood analysis. We retained our interest in identifying instructionally effective schools for the poor, but in addition we wanted to study the effects of schools on children having different social backgrounds. Such an inquiry would permit us to evaluate school contributions to educational outcomes independent of our ability to match schools on the basis of the socioeconomic characteristics of their pupils.

Summarizing and oversimplifying results, we found at least 55 effective schools in the Northeast quadrant of the EEOS. Our summary definition of school effectiveness required that each school eliminate the relationship between successful performance and family background. The effective schools varied widely in racial composition, per pupil expenditure, and other presumed determinants of school quality.

In our reanalysis of the EEOS, separate evaluation of the schools were made for subgroups of pupils of different races and home backgrounds. Schools were found to be consistently effective (or ineffective) in teaching subgroups of their populations that were homogeneous in race and economic condition. These schools were not found to be consistently effective in teaching children of differing economic condition and race. School effectiveness for a given level on Coleman's home items scale extended across racial lines. The prime factors that condition a school's instructional effectiveness appear to be principally economic and social, rather than racial.

Without seeking to match effective and ineffective schools on mean social background variables, we found that the schools that were instructionally effective for poor and black children were indistinguishable from the instructionally less effective schools on measures of pupil social background (mean father's and mother's education, category of occupation, percentage of white students, mean family size, and percentage of intact families). The large differences in performance between the effective and ineffective schools could not therefore be attributed to differences in the social class and family background of pupils enrolled in the schools. This finding is in striking contrast to that of other analysts of the EEOS, who have generally concluded that variability in performance levels from school to school is only minimally related to institutional characteristics.

A very great proportion of the American people believe that family background and home environment are principal causes of the quality of pupil performance. In fact, no notion about schooling is more widely held than the belief that the family is somehow a principal determinant of whether or not a child will do well in school. The popularity of that belief continues partly because many social scientists and opinion makers continue to espouse the belief that family background is a chief cause of the quality of pupil performance. Such a belief has the effect of absolving educators of their professional responsibility to be instructionally effective.

While recognizing the importance of family background in developing a child's character, personality, and intelligence, I cannot overemphasize my rejection of the notion that a school is relieved of its instructional obligations when teaching the children of the poor. I reject such a notion partly because I recognize the existence of schools that successfully teach basic school skills to all children. Such success occurs partly because these schools are determined to serve all their pupils without regard to family background. At the same time, these schools recognize the necessity of modifying curricular design, text selection, teaching strategy, etc., in response to differences in family background among pupils in the school. Our findings strongly recommend that all schools be held responsible for effectively teaching basic school skills to all children. We recommend that future studies of school and teacher effectiveness consider the stratification design as a means for investigating the separate relationship of programs and policies for pupils of differing family and social background. Information about individual student family background and social class is essential in our analysis if we are to disentangle the separate effects of pupil background and school social class makeup on pupil achievement. Moreover, studies of school effectiveness should be multivariate in character and employ longitudinal records of pupil achievement in a variety of areas of school learning.

The "Search for Effective Schools Project" has completed its analysis of social class, family background, and pupil performance for all Lansing, Michigan, pupils in grades three through seven.

We have identified five Lansing schools in which achievement seems independent of pupil social class. The achievement data are: local and normative; and state and criterion. We use both sets of data to identify schools in which all pupils are achieving beyond minimum objectives, including especially those children of low social class and poverty family background. We are now gathering similar data for Detroit pupils in the elementary grades in schools with pupil populations that are at least 15% poor.

The on-site study of Lansing's effective schools as compared with ineffective schools, begun in the 1978–79 school year, has been concluded. Our basic notions of the character and origin of effective and ineffective school differences derive from work we've already done in combination with ideas on school effects that I've held for a long time.[22] On the basis of the review of the literature in this paper, the earlier study in Detroit Model Cities of the "Effective Schools" project, and EEOS's Northeast quadrant data, I would offer the following about the distinguishing characteristics of schools that are instructionally effective for poor children.

What effective schools share is a climate in which it is incumbent on all personnel to be instructionally effective for all pupils. That is not, of course, a very profound insight but it does define the proper lines of research inquiry.

What ought to be focused on are questions such as: What is the origin of that climate of instructional responsibility; if it dissipates what causes it to do so; if it remains what keeps it functioning? Our tentative answers are these. Some schools are instructionally effective for the poor because they have a tyrannical principal who compels the teachers to bring all children to a minimum level of mastery of basic skills. Some schools are effective because they have a self-generating teacher corps that has a critical mass of dedicated people committed to be effective for all the children they teach. Some schools are effective because they have a highly politicized Parent Teacher Organization that holds the schools to close instructional account. The point here is to make clear that no one model explains school effectiveness for the poor or any other social class subset. Fortunately children know how to learn in more ways than we know how to teach, thus permitting great latitude in choosing instructional strategy. The great problem in schooling is that we know how to teach in ways that can keep some children from learning most anything, and we often choose to thus proceed when dealing with the children of the poor.

Thus, one of the cardinal characteristics of effective schools is that they are as anxious to avoid things that don't work as they are committed to implementing things that do.

What, then, are the most tangible and indispensable characteristics of effective schools? They have *strong administrative leadership* without which the disparate elements of good schooling can be neither brought together nor kept together. Schools that are instructionally effective for poor children have a *climate of expectation* in which no children are permitted to fall below minimum but efficacious levels of achievement. The school's *atmosphere is orderly* without being rigid, quiet without being oppressive, and generally conducive to the instructional business at hand. Effective schools get that way partly by making it clear that *pupil acquisition of basic school skills takes precedence over all other school activities.* When necessary, school energy and resources can be diverted from other business in furtherance of the fundamental objectives. The final effective school characteristic to be set down is that there must be some means by which *pupil progress can be frequently monitored.* These means may be as traditional as classroom testing on the day's lesson or as advanced as systemwide standardized measures. The point is that some means must exist in the school by which the principal and the teachers remain constantly aware of pupil progress in relationship to instructional objectives.

It seems to me therefore that what is left of this discussion are three declarative statements. We can whenever, and wherever we choose, successfully teach all children whose schooling is of interest to us. We already know more than we need to accomplish that task. Whether or not we do it must finally depend on how we feel about the fact that we haven't so far.

Now what is the import of this summary discussion for desegregation as a national strategy of educational equity? First, desegregation planners, for the most part, proceed on the basis of a set of premises that are far more akin to Coleman and Jencks than to the alternative premises I am here recommending. Unless that changes, desegregation plans can never yield the instructional gains to which black children are entitled. Second, demographic desegregation must take a backseat to instructional reform or we will remain frustrated by a continuing and widening gap between white and black pupil performance in desegregated schools. Finally, we must abandon the legal perspective that treats desegregation litigation as a matter solely of racial balance and assumes quality education will come with that balance. Surely, it must now be clear that black parents want effective schooling for their children and desegregation is useful to black parents if, and only if, it moves to that end.

There is no need to despair. The record is clear, our task undone, and all that is wanted is the will to use what is now known.

NOTES

1. J. Bolner and R. Shanley, *Busing: The Political and Judicial Process* (Praeger, 1974).
2. R. Edmonds, C. Cheng, and R. Newby, "Desegregation Planning and Educational Equity: Prospects and Possibilities," *Theory Into Practice* 17, no. 1, February 1978.
3. R. Edmonds, "Desegregation and Equity: Community Perspectives," *Harvard Graduate School of Education Association Bulletin* 19, no. 2, Winter, 1974–75.
4. Nancy H. St. John, *School Desegregation: Outcomes for Children* (Wiley, 1975).
5. J. S. Coleman, E. O. Campbell, C. J. Hobson, J. McPartland, A. M. Mood, F. D. Weinfeld, and R. L. York, *Equality of Educational Opportunity* (Washington, D.C.: U.S. Office of Education, National Center for Educational Statistics, 1966).
6. C. Jencks et al., *Inequality: A Reassessment of the Effect of Family and Schooling in America* (Basic Books, 1972).
7. "What the Research Studies Show," *The New York Times,* Sunday, November 13, 1977.
8. G. Weber, *Inner City Children Can Be Taught to Read: Four Successful Schools* (Washington, D.C.: Council for Basic Education, 1971), p. 30; H. A. Averch, S. J. Carroll, T. S. Donaldson, H. J. Kiesling, and J. Pincus, *How effective is schooling? A critical review and synthesis of research findings,* pp. 154–158 (Santa Monica, California: The Rand Corporation, 1972).
9. G. Weber, *Inner City Children Can Be Taught to Read.*
10. A. Jensen, "How Much Can We Boost IQ and Scholastic Achievement?" *Harvard Educational Review,* Winter, 1969.
11. State of New York, "School Factors Influencing Reading Achievement: A Case Study of Two Inner-City Schools" March 1974. State of New York Office of Education Performance Review.
12. Ibid., pp. vi and vii.
13. J. V. Madden, D. R. Lawson, and D. Sweet, *School Effectiveness Study: State of California,* 1976.
14. Ibid.
15. W. B. Brookover and L. W. Lezotte, "Changes in School Characteristics Coincident with Changes in Student Achievement," College of Urban Development of Michigan State University and the Michigan Department of Education, 1977.
16. Research Evaluation and Assessment Services of the Michigan Depart-

ment of Education, *Report of the 1974–75 Michigan Cost Effectiveness Study* (Capital Publications, 1976).

17. W. Brookover et al., "Elementary School Climate and School Achievement" (College of Urban Development of Michigan State University, 1976). This study has since been published as: *School Social Systems and Student Achievement: Schools Can Make a Difference* (New York: Praeger, 1979).

18. Brookover and Lezotte, "Changes in School Characteristics."

19. R. R. Edmonds and J. R. Fredericksen, "Search for Effective Schools: The Identification and Analysis of City Schools That Are Instructionally Effective for Poor Children" (Center for Urban Studies, Harvard University, Cambridge, Mass., 1978).

20. Larry Lezotte, Ronald Edmonds, and Gerson Ratner, *Remedy for School Failure to Equitably Deliver Basic School Skills* (Center for Urban Studies, Harvard University, Cambridge, Mass., 1974).

21. John Fredericksen, *School Effectiveness and Equality of Educational Opportunity* (Center for Urban Studies, Harvard University, Cambridge, Mass., 1975).

22. R. R. Edmonds, "Alternative Patterns for the Distribution of Social Services," *Equality and Social Policy*, ed. Walter Feinberg (University of Illinois Press, 1978).

CHAPTER EIGHT

It is, as the Chinese would say, a contradiction. The essays in this book provide a jurisprudential foundation, and a legally sound rationale, for moving beyond the arguably obsolete and certainly ineffective strategy of implementing *Brown* by reliance on racial-balance remedies. And yet many of the authors here have been expressing similar views for years without much discernible effect on courts, school boards, or civil rights policy makers.

Many who remain committed at all costs to school integration through racial assignments are motivated by the belief that a black school is, by definition, a bad school. It is appropriate before closing to both address this belief candidly, and attempt to firmly expose it as wrong.

More than a commitment to truth dictates this duty. An ever-increasing number of black parents, particularly those whose low economic status limits their schooling choices, are organizing in efforts to make the equal educational opportunity of *Brown* "real" within the schools that serve black communities.

For both those committed to integration via racial balance, and black parents who seek better black schools, the question is: how can *Brown* be used as the vehicle for providing effective schooling in mainly minority schools? This final chapter provides a general response that, it is hoped, will generate specific plans modelled to fit the diverse interests and needs of minority groups across the country.

124

A MODEL ALTERNATIVE
DESEGREGATION PLAN

BLACK SCHOOLS AND ACCEPTED TRUTHS

It is the conventional wisdom in this country that any public school whose student population is all or mainly black is presumptively a poor school. In such a school, according to the general understanding, learning takes second place to discipline, and teaching techniques are subordinated to rules designed to promote safety and order. Academic performance is low and absenteeism is high. Fighting and stealing are supposedly valued by students more than reading and writing, and teachers deserve, and often receive, "combat pay" merely for showing up and surviving, whether or not their students learn anything.

The belief that this model of the all-black school was the result of racial segregation motivated the litigation that led to *Brown*. For more than a quarter of a century, the hope that integration was the antidote for bad black schools fired the zeal of those committed to implementing *Brown* through racial balance remedies designed to eliminate every predominantly black school.

To a far larger extent than any of us would like, the definitively defined degradation in the archetype all-black school is, in fact, present at least to some degree in many schools that are all or mainly black. In such schools, particularly if they are located in urban areas, pupil performance as measured by standardized tests drops lower the longer students remain in school. Vandalism, teacher safety, and student discipline problems are the major concerns of school authorities. Out of necessity, young teachers may begin their careers in such schools, but their goal is to survive until they gain sufficient seniority to transfer to "better" (defined as mainly white) schools. When, as pointed out by Sara Lightfoot and Ron Edmonds, liberal social scientists attribute poor pupil performance in black schools to factors of disadvantage in

the home and community, school officials understandably, if not jus-
tifiably, quickly adopt this rationale to explain why so much in public
funds voted to all-black schools produces so little educational result.

The sense of low expectation in black schools is quickly transferred
from school performance to students and parents. As W. E. B. DuBois
pointed out years ago, blacks will often work and strive to integrate an
all-black school. When they fail, they sit back rather than exert similar
efforts to improve the quality of the all-black school. As a predictable
result, the school's performance soon falls to the low level predicted for
it. Interestingly enough, these beliefs are not significantly affected by
the existence of educationally effective black public schools, even during the pre-*Brown* era of segregation. Professor Thomas Sowell and
others have researched and written about the academic accomplishments made by blacks in segregated high schools like Dunbar, in
Washington, D.C.; Booker T. Washington, in Atlanta; Frederick
Douglass, in Baltimore; and McDonough, in New Orleans.[1] These
researchers have labored mightily, but usually in vain, to erase the
myth that the performance achieved in these schools was due to exceptional factors: The students were carefully selected from upper-class,
black families, or the teachers were Ph.D.s who could not find work
outside the segregated school system. Sowell has pointed out that black
superachievers, like Ralph Bunche, Charles Drew, Edward W. Brooke,
and William H. Hastie all graduated from Dunbar High School. Indeed, most black leaders over 40 years old and much of the black
middle-class are products of segregated schooling. None of these facts
does much to alter the belief that a black school—segregated or not—is,
of necessity, a bad school.

Periodically, the news media discovers an individual black school
that is functioning well. As this was written, much of the country's
educational community was hailing the accomplishments of a black
teacher in Chicago, Marva Collins, whose success in teaching young
black children to read classics has been reported on a nationwide
television program. Ms. Collins, disgusted with the public schools, took
her retirement money and opened a school in her home, where 30
pupils from grades one to eight quickly gained achievement in reading
and math that would be the envy of expensive and highly rated private
schools. Ms. Collins denied that there was anything special about her or
her children. She claimed that she believed the children could learn,
conveyed this belief, and insisted that they work to achieve. It was also
obvious that the parents of most of her children were involved in the
learning process. Nevertheless, both viewers and commentators hailed
Ms. Collins and her school as exceptional and nonreplicable.

Similar excitement has been generated by reports of superior achievement by black students in the Holy Angel Catholic School in Chicago, or the Reading Is Yours To Keep Program in Boston, the BUILD Academy in Buffalo, and Vernum Dei in Los Angeles. Each has been designated as an isolated phenomenon, remarkable in itself, but of little value for the massive problem of the typical black school.

With this attitude, it should not be a surprise to find that few serious studies have been undertaken to determine the characteristics of a successful black school. The studies undertaken and reported by Ron Edmonds indicating that dozens of inner-city public schools are performing well break new ground in a field in which most social science information about race and the schools has been committed to the minutiae of integration, where analytical microscopes must be used to observe academic progress by blacks in even the most carefully integrated schools. Indeed, these studies demand the conclusion reached by Nancy St. John that integration offers no guarantee of a quality education for black students. And yet the pursuit of integration to achieve this goal has not changed. It is significant and characteristic that in late 1979, civil rights attorneys moved the federal courts to reopen the Topeka, Kansas, school desegregation case with Linda Brown, the original plaintiff, once again involved, this time on behalf of her children. The resurrected *Brown* litigation speaks much for the persistence of those who believe even now that racial balance remedies are the answer. It also reveals, unfortunately, their rigidity and their unwillingness to face facts long plain to all who will see.

Along with Alan Freeman, I have argued here that, for a combination of social, political, and economic reasons, there is less likelihood that racial balance remedies can be enforced or even obtained today than they could have been a decade ago. There are those who will debate this conclusion. But that debate might be more meaningfully resolved if school systems on their own or those representing black parents urged the adoption of educationally oriented remedies like those contained in the Ron Edmonds article.

The week following the television program devoted to the Marva Collins School in Chicago, viewers wrote in urging that Ms. Collins be named Secretary of Education and that her teaching strategy be copied for use in other schools. White parents wrote of their admiration for learning levels that their children had not achieved in their schools. There is no doubt that, given an opportunity, many white parents would voluntarily enroll their children in schools like that run by Marva Collins. Thus, even for those who adhere to the belief that racial balance is the only appropriate outcome of *Brown,* it is likely that the establishment and maintenance of effective all-black schools is the best means of moving toward that goal.

ALTERNATIVE VISIONS IN OUTLINED FORM

The question remains: Is it possible to achieve throughout a school system the impressive performance that unusually talented and committed teacher/administrators have exhibited in individual black schools? I hope the answer is yes, but the justification for seeking alternative remedies in school desegregation cases is less the certainty that they will succeed than the reality that remedies relying on racial balance and busing are not working now and threaten further erosion of the equal educational opportunity goal in the future.

At the least, the possibility that individual examples of successful black schools can serve as models for court-ordered remedies is sufficiently strong to warrant a realistic trial. The ideal approach would call for plaintiffs' counsel in cases where school board liability for segregated schools has been imposed to seek educationally oriented remedies; but school desegregation litigation remains an expensive activity requiring skilled and persistent attorneys. Only a few civil rights organizations and the federal government have the necessary resources, and they remain committed to racial balance remedies. Thus, the initiative for alternative remedies must come from the courts or concerned parents' groups who are able to intervene in the litigation or otherwise influence the remedial process. In either case, the outline of an alternative plan process should involve several steps.

1.   Black Community Input

A major defect in civil rights strategy in the implementation of *Brown* has been the expectation that the racial balance remedy could be imposed in every school district regardless of the district's size, racial composition, resources, and, most important of all, the outlook and expectations of black parents. This is a serious mistake. To avoid it requires at the remedy stage at least a partial rescission by the court of the assumptions regarding the plaintiffs' adequacy as representatives of the class. Rather, as the district judge in the Atlanta school case did with some success,[2] several days of public hearings should be set at which community representatives and individual parents should be permitted to provide their views and suggestions about the desired composition and goals of the desegregation plan. Notice of these hearings should be carried in the media, but individual notice should be provided to civic and community groups and to black parents through written announcements distributed to the children by the schools.

If, as might occur in a small school district where the percentage of black students is also small, the response favors integration in the traditional manner, the court might proceed with the racial balance plan that probably would be urged by plaintiffs' counsel. Imposition of the plan after hearings urging its adoption would provide judges with the knowledge that the remedy actually was desired by those entitled to relief. In most large districts where the percentage of Blacks is also large, school improvement will likely be favored by both black parents and their community spokespersons. Both will be able to detail their problems with the public schools and the character of reform that they seek.

The value of public hearings is particularly important if the school district contains Spanish-speaking, Asian, or other minority groups. Such groups are often quite committed to improving the quality of schooling at the schools serving their residential areas. In all too many school desegregation cases, the rights and legitimate educational interests of these groups have been ignored or given low priority in the major battles between plaintiffs and school boards over the range and scope of racial balance and busing.

2.   Desegregation Plan Committee

Armed with the transcripts of testimony by the minority communities, the Court should appoint a small committee of three to five persons to draft an alternative desegregation plan. The committee should include:

- one or more educators with experience and proven success in effectively educating minority children in predominantly minority schools;
- one or more minority parents or generally recognized local spokespersons for minority parents' interests. If there is a sizeable Puerto Rican, Mexican-American, Asian, Native American, or other minority group, representatives from such groups should also be included.
- a lawyer knowledgeable in school desegregation law, but sympathetic to the idea of alternative desegregation plans could prove a helpful addition to the committee, but may prove difficult to find.
- a social scientist with insight and experience in racial issues would be a helpful addition to the committee.

3.   Necessary Plan Components

While the Desegregation Plan Committee should be given all possible leeway in their deliberations, a few, basic guidelines are necessary to insure that the plan submitted remains within the boundaries of what the *Brown* mandate could reasonably require. Thus:

- The plan should aim to bring minority schools up to the academic standards of mainly white schools in the district. Both black and white students in a given district may deserve more, but it is doubtful whether the equal educational opportunity standard in *Brown* enables the court to issue more far-reaching orders.
- The plan should place final responsibility for minority-school effectiveness on the school board. The mechanisms for achieving effective schools may differ, depending on local problems and the availability of resources, but the Committee should attempt to build into their plan the components recognized by Sara Lightfoot and Ron Edmonds in high-achieving black schools:

  a. Provision for strong, dynamic leadership with sufficient authority over selection and retention of teaching and administrative personnel to insure that credit or responsibility for the school's success or failure can be assessed fairly.

  b. Ample opportunity for black and other minority parents to be involved in their children's schooling. This may include provision for participation in planning and policymaking but should insure parental cooperation in, and understanding of, the teaching and learning process. This may involve periodic visits by teachers to their students' homes, or the use of teaching materials requiring parental involvement. The mechanisms may vary, but effective teaching at school usually requires active, parental support and often participation.

- The plan should insure that minority schools receive at least the same funding as the white schools deemed "best" by the school district. Because 75 to 80 percent of a school's budget goes to salaries, and because the most experienced and thus most highly paid teachers generally percolate up to the "best" white schools, this resource equalization standard should insure that black and other minority schools have that share of the district's funds needed to provide quality teachers, smaller classroom enrollments, and perhaps specialized teaching materials needed to meet the equal educational opportunity standard usually after long years of neglect and frequently unequal funding. If state liability can be established, the court can order the state to contribute funds to cover the cost of remedial programs.

- The plan must include a majority to minority provision under which any child assigned to a school where his or her race is in the majority has the absolute right to a transfer to the closest available school where the child's race is in the minority. Transportation where distances require will be provided by the school board. Regardless of the nonimpressive results in many integrated schools, or the expectations for academic gain in the mainly black schools under the alternative plan, black parents (whites will seldom seek to exercise this option) who wish to have their children attend mainly white schools should have that right.

- The plan should make clear that while this is an alternative to a racial balance plan, it is no less based on the constitutional necessity of remedying basic rights of black children long violated by school board policies. The remediation process must thus take precedence over seniority, assignment, transfer and promotion arrangements based on contract, collective bargaining agreement, or board policy and practice.

- The plan should provide for ongoing monitoring of the plan's implementation and functioning either by the Desegregation Plan Committee or by a referee to be appointed by the court. Provision for periodic reports focused on the plan's educational effectiveness should be made by the school board. The plan must make clear that the board's failure to administer the plan in good faith and with priority effort will result in receivership proceedings, contempt citations, or similarly drastic remedies.

4.   Discretionary Plan Components

Needs may vary from district to district, but alternative desegregation plans may include provision for bilingual and bicultural courses, vocational training, and specialized student counselling. The plan may call for new standardized testing measures, and may require adoption of a new or revised disciplinary procedure intended to correct the disproportionate numbers of black children in most school districts who are suspended or expelled. Some desegregation plans, notably Boston, have included requirements that the school board seek assistance from major businesses and colleges in the area. Both resources can be helpful in providing job training, and reinforcing teaching ranks, but the responsibility for raising black schools to a level of equal educational effectiveness must remain with the school board.

5.   Judicial Approval Process

After the Desegregation Plan Committee submits its final plan to the court, both plaintiffs and defendants must be given an opportunity to object to the plan's provisions and suggest amendments, additions, or substitute plans. At a hearing on the plan, the court should appoint legal counsel capable of, and willing to, represent the interests of those who support the alternative plan. In some cases, intervenors representing black parents may be able to fulfill this role. Usually though, the litigation will have proceeded to the remedy stage with the major issue focused on the appropriateness of busing and racial balance. Thus, the court should request counsel for the alternative plan to gather and present additional evidence to prove that school board policies are responsible in whole or part for the academic deficiencies in black schools that alternative plan components are intended to correct. Additional discovery procedures may be required to present this proof.

Where plaintiffs' counsel in earlier phases of the litigation gave priority to proving policies that brought on or continued segregation in the various schools, alternative plan counsel should seek answers to questions like the following:

- Did the school board approve and maintain teacher and administrative personnel assignment policies after they knew or should have known that such policies would result in the migration of the most experienced and capable teachers from black to white schools with a concurrent loss of teacher effectiveness in black schools?
- What changes in principals or other supervisory personnel have been made to overcome the achievement gap between black and white schools?
- What special efforts have been made with reading and math programs specifically designed for poor, black children; or if minority children come from non-English speaking families, are appropriate bilingual and bicultural programs in use?
- Are educational programs designed to insure the involvement of minority parents in both school policymaking and in the ongoing education of their children?
- Are course offerings in mainly black schools equal in number and quality to those offered in white schools, and are the course offerings in black schools specifically designed to meet the educational needs of black students?
- Are measures of achievement, including standards for failure, promotion, and graduation fair as applied to black and other minority children?
- Does the school system designate a disproportionate number of black and other minority children as educationally handicapped and, if so, what is the effectiveness of programs prescribed for such children?
- Does the school system discipline through corporal punishment,

suspensions, and expulsions a percentage of black and other minority children higher than the percentage of such children in the public schools?

- Is the percentage of students who drop out or otherwise fail to graduate from the system's mainly black schools higher than the percentage of nongraduates from mainly white schools?
- Are state and local expenditures at schools serving mainly black and other minority children at least equal to expenditures at schools of similar size serving mainly white children?

In preparing legal arguments based on shortcomings in the school system revealed in responses to questions similar to those just suggested, counsel for the alternative plan may use some or all of the following precedents to good effect:

- *Milliken* v. *Bradley II*, 433 U.S. 267 (1977). The Supreme Court approved a series of wide-ranging "educational components," including programs in remedial reading and communications skills, comprehensive in-service teacher training, revised testing, and counselling and career guidance. The programs substituted in part for racial balance remedies rejected as impractical in Detroit's 80 percent black district. Because of its responsibility for the system's segregation, the state was ordered to help defray the costs of the remedial programs.
- *Lau* v. *Nichols*, 414 U.S. 563 (1974). The Supreme Court found that Title VI of the Civil Rights Act of 1964, requires that school systems receiving federal funds rectify in some appropriate fashion the English language deficiencies of Chinese children so that they may receive equality of educational treatment in schools where the curriculum is taught in English. The same conclusion was reached as to Spanish-surnamed students in *Serna* v. *Portales Municipal Schools*, 499 F.2d 1147 (10th Cir. 1974).
- *Martin Luther King Elementary School Children* v. *Ann Arbor School District Board*, 473 F. Supp. 1371, (E.D. Mich. 1979). A district court construed the 1974 Equal Educational Opportunity Act, 20 U.S.C. §1703(f), as forbidding state denial of equal educational opportunity on account of race by failing to utilize known methods of overcoming language barriers faced by students coming from homes and communities where black English is spoken. The schools need not teach black English, but teachers must understand its existence, the learning barriers it poses, and teach black children code switching skills in connection with reading standard English that are appropriate in the light of existing knowledge on the subject.
- *Larry P.* v. *Riles*, —— F. Supp. ——, 48 U.S.L.R. 2298 (Oct. 30,

1979). A district court found that California's use of an unvalidated IQ test, i.e., a standardized placement test that did not provide accurate information on the abilities of black children and resulted in a grossly disproportionate number of black children being assigned to "educable mentally retarded" classes is in violation of federal statutes, including Title VI of the 1964 Civil Rights Act. The court enjoined the state from using any standardized intelligence tests for the placement of black children in educable mentally retarded classes without the court's prior approval.

- *Debra P.* v. *Turlington,* 474 F. Supp. 244, (M.D. Fla., 1979). A district court held that application of a Florida statute limiting receipt of a standard high school diploma to those students able to pass a "functional literacy" test violates the equal protection rights of black students who attended racially segregated public schools during the first four years of public schooling. The failure rate of black students on the test was disproportionately high, and the court, in enjoining the state from requiring test passage as a condition of graduation for four years, found that it perpetuates past purposeful discrimination against black students, particularly since their education was controlled by the state, and they had no notice at the time of instruction in the functional literacy skills that such skills must be learned prior to graduation from a Florida public school.

SUMMARY IN QUESTION AND ANSWER FORM

It is likely that even those readers who are both deeply concerned about the slow pace of school desegregation, and sufficiently impressed by this presentation of alternative remedies to recognize their educational potential, are not without questions, reservations, and perhaps skepticism about the wisdom of altering the thrust of the decades-long movement to implement the *Brown* decision. In recognition of these reservations, I am concluding this discussion with a sampling of typical questions and answers presented at lectures and writings on alternative school remedies.

Q. Isn't your alternative remedy really a regression back to "separate but equal" schools available to black children prior to 1954?

A. No. From a constitutional standpoint, it was as Charles Lawrence so ably argued in his essay, a legal as well as societal impossibility to provide equality in schools that blacks were required by law to attend, in a system where such attendance was a badge of inferiority. Given their subordinate positions, it was all but impossible for blacks to insure the provision of equal resources to black schools. *Brown* is significant because it ended the legal subordination of blacks, removed the barriers that prevented blacks from going to school with whites, and made it possible for black parents to gain an equal educational opportunity for their children wherever those children attended school. To date, the major priority in implementing *Brown* has been placed on gaining an equal educational opportunity for black children attending predominantly white or integrated schools. In some districts this was and is an appropriate priority and it should continue. The alternative remedies discussed here are intended to enable the parents, community groups, and their legal counsel to suggest procedures and techniques by which priority can be given to implementing *Brown* in those schools that remain, or have become, mainly black. The key distinctions between these schools and those existing in the "separate but equal" era, are parental choice and the potential for educational effectiveness.

Q. But what about the educational values of an integrated school experience? The Supreme Court has interpreted the Brown *decision as mandating the maximum reasonable integration of schools. Doesn't the alternative plan ignore these decisions?*

A. In decisions where plaintiffs sought racial balance-oriented relief, the Supreme Court has indicated that the racial identifiability of schools should be erased, has permitted relatively long-distance busing to facilitate this goal, and has indicated that the retention of one-race schools creates a presumption that the school board has not carried out its responsibilities under *Brown*. The fact is that in most large districts where a large percentage of black students attend schools, it is no longer possible, as I discussed in further detail in my essay, to provide integrated assignments. Moreover, the value of alternative remedies depends on the dual assumptions discussed by several essays in this book: (1) that most black parents want their children to obtain an effective education as opposed to an integrated education and have sent their children to mainly white schools in the belief and hope that an effective education could best be obtained there; (2) that a meaningful integrated, school experience will become possible when white parents, recognizing the academic quality of mainly black schools, voluntarily send their children to these black schools.

Q. Hasn't the school desegregation movement been premised on the idea that "green follows white," that is, the money in the public schools follows the white students, and that blacks must enroll their children with white children in order to get the quality of education the school system will provide for the whites?

A. That strategy seemed a viable approach, but experience over the years indicates that to the extent school officials gave priority to the needs of white children, they continued to do so even in desegregated schools. Extra money for special programs with better, higher-paid teachers follows white students into special, upper-track classes even within integrated schools, where most blacks are trapped in lower-track, generally ineffective and less expensive course offerings. Again, in most large urban school districts, black children cannot follow whites who have moved to the suburbs or to private schools.

Q. What makes you think you are more qualified to set school desegregaton policies than the leadership and lawyers for the NAACP, Legal Defense Fund, and the ACLU, all of whom continue to support racial balance remedies?

A. I don't claim superior qualifications, but I have worked in one aspect or another of school desegregation for more than twenty years. While a staff lawyer of the Legal Defense Fund from 1960 to 1966, I personally handled or supervised almost 300 school desegregation cases. Later, I was Deputy Director of HEW's Office for Civil Rights during the formulation of its first school desegregation guidelines. During the last ten years, I have written extensively in law journals on the subject. In one article, I suggested that civil rights lawyers are so committed to racial balance remedies, they fail to recognize that their clients most want effective schooling for their children. This article, "Serving Two Masters: Integration Ideals and Client Interests in School Desegregation Litigation," 85 *Yale L. Journal* 470 (1976), was not received well by my former civil rights colleagues, a fact that has brought me much sadness. But I don't think representatives of poor, black people can afford the luxury of rigid adherence to one strategy when it is clear both that the strategy is no longer working, and that other potentially more viable strategies are available.

Q. Aren't you afraid that your alternative remedy will involve the courts too deeply in educational matters and further sacrifice the traditional, local control of school policymaking to nonelected judges who have little or no educational expertise?

A. This is a problem, but blacks in general have too little economic or political power to effect the needed public school reforms on their own. The courts are not an ideal vehicle for social reform, but often they are the only agency of government sufficiently sensitive enough to both the law and the real self-interest of the society to make a moderate amount of change possible. In the school desegregation area moreover, the courts have already become deeply involved in educational processes through their efforts to enforce racial balance-oriented remedies. The alternative remedies suggested here would not increase that involvement but rather would move it into directions where the courts, if the Supreme Court's 9-0 decision in the second Detroit case (*Milliken* v. *Bradley*) are any indication, would prefer to go. In addition, to the extent that alternative remedies provide structures that may enable black parents to be involved in school policymaking and in the ongoing schooling of their children, they increase the likelihood that courts can eventually withdraw from the school desegregation process. This has not been the case in litigation aimed at achieving racial balance.

Q. Racial balance remedies do involve standards that can easily be measured by noting the percentage of black and white students attending each school in the system. Isn't the weakness of your alternative remedies the absence of numerical standards by which to measure progress?

A. No. The courts, school boards, and concerned parents can utilize standard test-score results to measure the improvement in effectiveness of black schools. They might also note dropout rates; disciplinary statistics; the percentage of graduates going on to college, training programs, and/or into full time employment; and similar measures. In addition, those effective black schools that are the models for the alternative remedies discussed here are characterized by a high level of morale and strong feelings of competence evident in talking to teachers and students, and by an obvious degree of satisfaction on the part of parents and the community.

Q. In the final analysis, isn't effective education dependent in substantial part on motivation of students and teachers, which reflects their knowledge that the schooling effort will pay off in postgraduation jobs and money, or college admissions that will eventually pay off in even better jobs with more money? Don't the problems in most schools serving poor black children stem from the recognition by both teachers and pupils that educational efforts won't help them get jobs?

A. In fact, there are jobs for blacks and whites who have the needed qualifications and skills. There are fewer and fewer jobs for those with no education or skills. It is perhaps easy for ghetto children to confuse the two situations since they come in contact with so many unemployed blacks who are unemployable because of the marginal educations they obtained. An important role in all black schools located in poor communities is to clarify this distinction, and make clear the opportunities that are available to those with skills and education. A part of this task is to lift the sights of black children about both their opportunities and their ability to take advantage of these opportunities. This requires constantly reiterating in many ways the children's self-worth. It is not accidental that Reverend Jesse Jackson repeats over and over at his meetings with black students the phrase, "You are somebody." The televised report on Marva Collins' school in Chicago showed her spending a great deal of time telling her students that they could excel through work. This is one of several elements in an effective education that perhaps need not be emphasized in middle-class schools where children see success at home and in their communities. It deserves priority attention in mainly black schools.

Q. If you believe so thoroughly in the educational potential of black schools, why do you and so many other middle-class blacks send your children to mainly white public or private schools? Aren't you espousing a double standard?

A. No. All parents want their children to obtain the best possible education. My children attend neighborhood schools that have good educational reputations and happen to be mainly white. Were I living in an area within even long-distance busing of an effective all-black school, I would prefer that my children attend that school. Moreover, they would prefer to attend such a school. There is a subtle but real harassment faced by students in mainly white schools that is manifested by a low academic expectation from at least some teachers, and a general sense of minority subordination to white interests that is present in even the most conscientiously run white schools. The difficulties that these problems create for black children, whether poor or middle class, may be seen as good preparation for life in a white world, but all blacks receive plenty of such preparation in their day-to-day experiences, and even in reading the newspaper or watching television. What black children do not receive is the spiritual uplift and self-assurance that come from being a part of an institution where persons like themselves are in charge, and where the rank and file of students and teachers share their interests, views, and experiences. This value would not be diluted and indeed might be enhanced by the presence of 10 to 20 percent white students who could offer the positive values of interracial interaction without the negative aspects of white control that inevitably occur in settings where the racial balance is predominantly white.

Q. How do you know alternative remedies will work? Racial balance remedies have their weaknesses, but the courts have supported them for almost two decades. If you convince them to shift to alternative remedies, and they are failures, won't the educational potential of the Brown *decision be irrevocably lost?*

A. There is always that risk, but the potential of *Brown* is now being dissipated through futile adherence to racial balance remedies that are increasingly hard to obtain. More importantly, black parents are increasingly disenchanted with remedies that have increased their educational burden without improving the quality of schooling provided their children. Alternative remedies seek to translate the desire of black parents for educationally effective schools into school policies that can gain judicial approval. They provide a vehicle for continuing the Supreme Court's and the country's commitment to the equal educational opportunity mandate of *Brown*.

There are no surefire formulas for educating poor children in this country. When those poor children are nonwhite, the barriers to good schooling are increased. Given this unhappy fact, lawyers, judges, educators and others in policy-influencing positions should exert every effort to insure that minority parents are not denied the greatest possible choice in their selection of schools. To assert, as some lower court judges have done, that black children must be assigned so as to racially balance schools whether or not their parents approve of such assignments is to exert under the rubric of remedy that character of racial dominance that was the essential evil of the separate but equal era. To justify this assertion of dominance by citation to the *Brown* decision reduces this historic precedent to the status occupied by so many civil rights laws that symbolize equality, but offer no means by which those who need it most can enjoy its benefits.

NOTES

1. Sowell, *Black Excellence: The Case of Dunbar High School,* THE PUBLIC INTEREST, No. 35, 1 (Spring 1974); Sowell, *Patterns of Black Excellence,* THE PUBLIC INTEREST, No. 43, 26 (Spring 1976).
2. Calhoon v. Cook, 362 F. Supp. 1249, 1250–51 (N.D. Ga. 1973). In addition to the general media coverage given the settlement proposal (providing for only limited pupil desegregation in the then 82-percent-black-district in exchange for the board's promise to hire a number of blacks in top administrative positions, including a black superintendent of schools), the court ordered publication of the pending settlement plan on a daily basis for two weeks in local papers, and required that copies be available at the school board office and at centrally located schools in each ward.

    In addition to testimony by the parties, local officials, and other interested parties at a special hearing, the court also considered formal and informal written communications, including petitions signed by several thousand blacks urging approval of the settlement plan. The court's approval was affirmed on appeal. 522 F.2d 717 (5th Cir. 1975), petitions for rehearing were denied. 525 F.2d 1203 (5th Cir. 1975).

Index